EASY

CONTAINER COMBOS:
VEGETABLES
& FLOWERS

By Pamela Crawford

For anyone who has ever killed a plant!

Pictured: Mustard greens, chrysanthemums (edible flowers) and ornamental cabbages

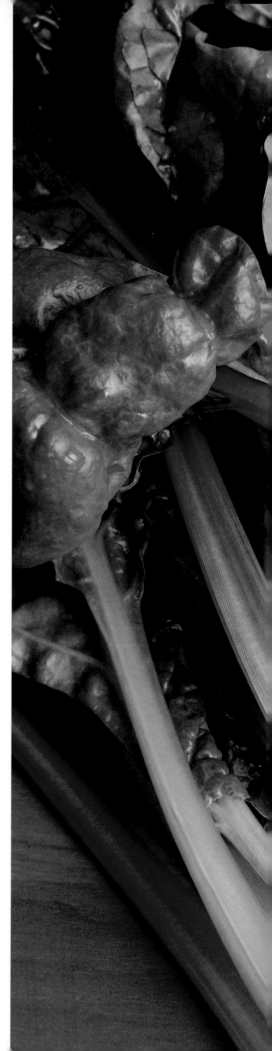

Where to Buy "Easy Container Combos: Vegetables & Flowers" Book:

The book is available through many garden centers and book sellers. It is also available through www.kinsmangarden.com and www.amazon.com. To locate your nearest source or place an order with the publisher, contact us at:

Color Garden Publishing
1353 Riverstone Parkway, Canton, GA 30114
Phone: 561-371-2719   Fax: 770-720-9719
Web site: www.easygardencolor.com
Email: info@easygardencolor.com

Credits:

Author: Pamela Crawford
Research Assistants: Kathy Stose and Barbara Hadsell
Cover Design and Graphic Design Assistance: Elaine Weber Designs, Inc. (www.ewdlogos.com)
Proofreader: Barbara Iderosa, Best Editing Service, Lake Worth, Florida
Horticultural Consultant: Lois Chaplin
Photography: All photos by Pamela Crawford except for the following:
Alaettin Yildirim, cucumbers, p. 45; Amlet, cucumber flower, pp. 95, 117, 153; Anders Sjoman, peppers, p. 160; Anette Linea Rasmussen, turnip greens, p. 155; Anna 1311, corn, pp. 19, 20; Baloncici, artichokes, p. 19; Brina Donaldson, squash, pp. 16, 25; Barbara Dudzinska, pizza, p. 143; Coulor, arugula, p. 142; Denis Nata, cucumber p. 117. Dmitriy Bryndin, cabbage, pp. 10, 16, 22, 25, 85; Dwight Smith, eggplant, p. 154; Efirm, tomatoes, p. 109; Elena Ioachim, eggplant, pp. 14, 22, 25; Elena Moiseeva, tomatoes, p. 9; Feverpitch, beans, pp. 12, 24, 25,144; Freddy Eliassen, arugula, pp. 12, 85; Hintau Aliaksel, tomatoes, p. 164; Historisches Auge Falf Feltz, asparagus, pp. 17, 18; Igor Norman, cantaloupe on pages 17, 18; Inta Eihame, cucumber, pp. 84, 96, 153; Kheng Guan Toh, broccoli, pp. 16, 25, 146; Jukubski, zucchini, pp. 45, 163; Larry Korb, cauliflower, pp. 10, 17, okra pp. 15, 25, 31, 75, 158; Lepos Hor, peas, pp. 116, 25, 159; Lois Chaplin, Bonnie Plants, 3 photos of peat pots, p. 41, tomatoes, p. 119; Marie C. Fields, pumpkins pp. 17, 18; Montenegro, peppers p. 161; Pefkos, spinach, pp. 13, 24, 85, 162; Piotr Marcinski, arugula, p. 143; Ronfromyork, brussel sprouts, pp. 16, 25, 147; carrots, p. 17, peppers on pp. 25, 75, 85; Sandi Mako, yellow squash, p. 163; Simbiot, tomatoes, pp. 8, 15, 25, 44, 165; Svetlana Lukienko, vegetable grouping, p. 37; Tonya Emsh, Swiss chard, pp. 2, 3, 16, 24, 150; Vitelle, Brussel sprouts, p. 147; Trudy Wilkerson, watermelon, pp. 16, 25, 166; Worytko Pawel, cucumbers, pp. 14, 25, 152.
Printing: Asianprinting.com, Korea

Published by Color Garden, Inc., Canton, GA. First printing: 2010
Library of Congress Catalog Card Number pending

ISBN 10: 0-9712220-9-6
ISBN 13: 978-0-9712220-9-0

Cover photo of container by author; Cheryl E. Davis, okra; Sandra Caldwell, chili peppers, eggplant; Stefano Tiraboschi, tomatoes, red/yellow peppers; LockStockBob, broccoli; Arnaud Weisser, cucumber. Back cover and inside back cover photographs by Amber Eberly.
Right: Swiss chard; photo by Tanya Emsh

Contents

Vegetable Trials Were Tough, but We Did Find Easy Ones

When people ask me what I do, I tell them that I write gardening books. Most people tell me they routinely kill plants. I am writing this book for them.

As a gardener, I initially had more bad luck than good. Many of my plants died because of one blunder after another. But, I just loved flowers and this lead me to dedicate my career to determining which plants were easy. I received a master's degree in landscape architecture, which included a master's thesis in plants that were well adapted to the environment, or easy plants. Landscape and ornamental plants, not vegetables.

Shortly afterwards, I started a nursery to grow plants for my landscaping customers. I moved into a house on the nursery grounds and quickly started my dream - large trial gardens that would mimic the average yard. I had no automatic watering system - the plants got water once a week if it didn't rain. None of them were sprayed with pesticides. I trimmed them once a year, at the most. None of them were pampered in the least.

At the end of ten years, 2500 different ornamental and landscape plants (no vegetables at all!) had been planted in my gardens. 2300 were dead. Many would look upon this low survival rate as a complete failure. I looked upon it as a great success because I had 200 great plants! I proceeded to write five books about landscape plants and three on container gardening before beginning vegetable trials.

I am addicted to flowers and have quite a bit of experience with them at this point. Vegetables are another story. I had never grown any before deciding to write this book. I thought I was a good enough gardener to have great success right from the start. But, success did not come easily. Out of 1768 plants in 221 containers, 1376 failed. Most of the containers we initially planted didn't do well because of the following:

Lois Chaplin, of Bonnie Plants, was a tremendous help with our trial gardens for vegetables.

✿ We didn't know enough about the ultimate size of the plant to use them correctly. For example, we planted yellow squash as edge plants with tomatoes in the center. The squash smothered the tomatoes.

✿ We planted vegetables in the wrong seasons. Brussels sprouts, for example, grow in cool weather, and we planted them in late spring in Georgia, when it was too hot.

✿ We weren't aware of the degree that vegetables would hide under leaves and completely missed harvesting some because we didn't know they were there.

✿ We planted too many varieties in one pot. Once we figured out how to keep it simple, we had much more success.

✿ Since the flowers we grew didn't get many bugs, we were inexperienced in spraying and had quite a few squash and cucumbers die from downy mildew for three reasons: we neglected to cut off the affected leaves, didn't spray religiously each week, and didn't spray the bottom of the leaves.

✿ Luckily, we started working with Lois Chaplin of Bonnie Plants (one of the largest vegetable growers in the country). Lois is an expert on vegetables and turned our project around. With her help and the sheer size of our trials, we ended up learning how to grow easy vegetables that look great! I hope our failures will help your success!

Our trial gardens in July. When you mix vegetables and flowers, the flowers show up much more than the vegetables. We actually missed harvesting some vegetables because we didn't know they were there! Use this book to avoid such mistakes.

These cucumber plants bore 23 fruit that were next to impossible to see unless you looked under the leaves.

The eggplant in this basket bore 15 fruit, but the flowers were much more noticeable.

These tomato plants bore 32 fruit that were somewhat easy to see.

Thank You To...

Bill Funkhouser, Kathy Stose, and Tammy Brogan holding up a backdrop we used on pages 42 and 97.

Barbara Hadsell

Elaine Golob Weber

Michele Kinsman

Graham Kinsman

Van Chaplin and Steve Bender of Southern Living with the author.

Katie Leslie, of the Atlanta Journal Constitution, for giving me the idea for this book.

Barbara Hadsell, my assistant, who has worked for years on preparation, marketing, and presentations for all of our books.

Kathy Stose, another key assistant, who helped design, plant, and maintain the containers. Kathy also shopped for plants and designed many of the sets we used for photography.

Lois Chaplin of Bonnie Plants, for her constant technical support. Lois also arranged for Bonnie Plants to supply most of the vegetables in this book - all of which were in season!

Van Chaplin (Senior Photographer) and Steve Bender (Senior Writer) of Southern Living. They visited twice while the trials were underway and offered invaluable advice.

Rambo Plants of Georgia for many flowering plants as well as ornamental vegetables.

Tom Oswald of JAM'n Designs (www.jamndesigns.com) and Pottery Land (www.potterylandusa.com) for many of the gorgeous containers.

Ray French of Floragem for many, many plants, including the spectacular Sunpatiens shown on pages 90, 114, and 124.

Tammy Brogan, a friend and helper, who assisted quite a bit with planting, maintaining, and setting up the containers for photography.

Bill Funkhouser, a house guest, who is also a plant expert. Every time he came for a visit, we roped him into helping us as well.

Phyllis Long of Redbud Lane Nursery (www.redbudlanenursery.com), Holly Springs, Georgia, for many plants as well as technical information.

Elaine Weber, the graphic designer, worked enthusiastically with me on some very tight deadlines.

Graham Kinsman and his wife, Michele, who worked with me for over two years to develop the side-planted baskets shown throughout the book.

Buying Information for Side-Planted Containers

From garden centers
Go to www.sideplanting.com to find a list of garden centers near you. This is a great choice because you can pick up the plants and potting mix at the same time.

Online
Go to www.kinsmangarden.com for retail and www.kinsmanwholesale.com for wholesale.

Phone
1-800-733-4146 for retail orders or
1-800-733-5613 for wholesale orders.

USDA Plant Hardiness Map

AVERAGE ANNUAL MINIMUM TEMPERATURE		
Temperature (°C)	Zone	Temperature (°F)
-45.6 and Below	1	Below -50
-42.8 to -45.5	2a	-45 to -50
-40.0 to -42.7	2b	-40 to -45
-37.3 to -40.0	3a	-35 to -40
-34.5 to -37.2	3b	-30 to -35
-31.7 to -34.4	4a	-25 to -30
-28.9 to -31.6	4b	-20 to -25
-26.2 to -28.8	5a	-15 to -20
-23.4 to -26.1	5b	-10 to -15
-20.6 to -23.3	6a	-5 to -10
-17.8 to -20.5	6b	0 to -5
-15.0 to -17.7	7a	5 to 0
-12.3 to -15.0	7b	10 to 5
-9.5 to -12.2	8a	15 to 10
-6.7 to -9.4	8b	20 to 15
-3.9 to -6.6	9a	25 to 20
-1.2 to -3.8	9b	30 to 25
1.6 to -1.1	10a	35 to 30
4.4 to 1.7	10b	40 to 35
4.5 and Above	11	40 and Above

Hawaii

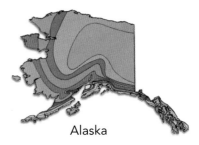

Alaska

The country is divided into zones based on minimum temperatures. Plants are classified by these zone numbers to determine where they can grow based on the lowest temperature they can take.

USDA Miscellaneous Publication No. 1475. Issued January 1990. Authored by Henry M. Cathey while Director, U.S. National Arboretum.

Edited, formatted and prepared for the US National Arboretum web site by Ramon Jordan, March 1998 & Revised March 2001 U.S. National Arboretum, Agricultural Research Service, U.S. Department of Agriculture, Washington, DC 20002 Special thanks to Jody Stuart and Scott Bauer, ARS Information Staff

Chapter 1

Foolproof
Container Growing

This chapter covers information needed to successfully choose and grow easy vegetables in containers. Don't miss pages 10 and 11 for a synopsis of the most important growing tips covered in this chapter. Here are the key points:

✿ Use the right materials.
1. Potting mix
2. Containers
3. Vegetables: Be sure you know these four qualities before buying:
    A. Mature size of the vegetable in containers
    B. How many vegetables you will harvest from each plant
    C. The vegetables' planting season
    D. If the vegetable is easy to grow in containers

✿ Plant and maintain vegetables properly.
1. Light
2. Planting techniques
3. Planting Jiffy (peat) pots
4. Planting bean seeds
3. Watering
4. Supporting vegetables
5. Pest control
6. Harvesting

✿ Take this book with you when you go to the garden center (pages 48 to 49). Use this book as a reference so that you will be sure to avoid all the problems I had!

Eight Easy Ways to Kill...

Buy the Wrong Plants.

Cauliflower tastes great but can be difficult to grow.

Most beginners buy plants that don't meet their expectations simply because they don't understand the plant's flowering habits - or the plant is an erratic performer.

Take this book with you to your garden center. Look up the flowers and vegetables in the index, and read about them prior to buying the plants. 'Easy Container Gardens' is a good choice to take with you as well. More flowers are referenced in that book.

You need to know how large a vegetable plant gets, how easy it is to grow in containers, when to plant it, and how many vegetables it will produce prior to buying it. The last chapter of this book includes this information.

Buy the Wrong Potting Mix.

Don't skimp on your potting mix. Good potting mix costs a little bit more, but makes all the difference. Plants grow larger and live longer with quality potting mix. Do not buy topsoil, garden soil, or potting soil for containers. It is too heavy, and the plants may rot and die quickly.

Look for a brand name you trust. Peters, Miracle Grow, Lambert's, and Fafard (along with many others) offer top-quality, potting mix.

Buy the Wrong Fertilizer.

I have killed plants with fertilizers several times. However, plants need nutrients, and fertilizer is an easy way to provide them. It hasn't been easy to choose the right one.

After years of mistakes and unhealthy plants, I discovered the fertilizer on page 36. It worked so well, without destroying anything in the process, that I put my name on it!

Plant in the Wrong Season.

Vegetables either like it warm or cool. Cabbages (right), for example, are cool-season vegetables, and if you plant them in the wrong season, they will not do well. I made this mistake several times and lost quite a few plants because of it.

See page 22 for listings of warm- and cool-season vegetables. The last chapter of this book gives much more detail about each vegetable.

Vegetables and Flowers.

Water Incorrectly.

Like people, plants need water to live. However, if you give them too much, they drown and die. If you give them too little, they die of thirst. Luckily, knowing when and how much to water is quite easy. See pages 38 to 40 for this information.

Most vegetables need a lot of water, but you can drown them just the same. Look for signs of wilting, or dry potting mix, before watering.

Left: See page 23 for more info on this combo.

Pile Potting Mix around the Stem of the Plant.

If potting mix or organic mulch comes into contact with the stem of many plants, the stem can rot, killing the plant (except for tomatoes). It is quite easy to avoid this plight by simply planting the plants a little a bit higher, as shown in the drawing.

To help retain water, some people like to put organic mulch on top of the potting mix after they have planted a container. This method works fine on large plants, like azaleas or ti plants, provided you don't pile the mulch up around the stem. However, on small plants, like impatiens or lettuce, it is quite difficult to mulch without harming the plant.

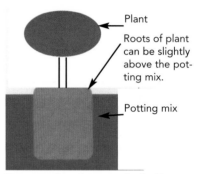

Plant

Roots of plant can be slightly above the potting mix.

Potting mix

Proper planting method: Roots can be slightly above the potting mix to avoid stem rot.

Plant in a Pot without Holes in the Bottom.

If your pots don't have holes in the bottom for drainage, the plants will die (unless the pot is specially designed for self watering). See page 29 to learn how to drill holes in the bottom of pots.

Luckily, most pots come with holes in the bottom. If you see one you want to buy that doesn't have holes, ask the salesperson if he/she will drill them for you. Many garden centers offer that service.

Give the Plant the Wrong Amount of Light.

Different plants need different amounts of light. A tomato (shown) likes sun, while lettuce takes more shade. But, how much sun is enough for sun plants? The rule of thumb is a minimum of six hours of direct sun every day. In other words, if your tomato just gets two hours of sun, with shade the rest of the day, it will not do well.

Most vegetables need a full six hours of sun per day. If they get less than that, they will not perform well. However, some cool-season, leafy vegetables (arugula, kale, lettuce, mustard greens, spinach, and Swiss chard) can get by with partial shade. See pages 24 to 25 as well as the individual plant profiles in the last chapter of this book for more specifics.

Easiest Vegetables: Just Add Water!

1ST

If you have never tried growing vegetables, start with one of these. If planted correctly, these blue ribbon vegetables seldom require anything but water! Be sure to follow these simple guidelines:

❀ Use potting mix (not potting soil, top soil, or garden soil) with a brand name you trust.

❀ Use the fertilizer decribed on page 36.

❀ Be sure the pot has holes in the bottom (page 13).

❀ Don't bury the plant too deep (page 29).

❀ Plant in the right amount of light and in the correct season, which varies per plant. Check the individual plant profiles in the last chapter of this book for specifics.

❀ Water correctly (pages 38 to 40).

Arugula	Beans	Collards

❀ Sometimes classed as an herb, I'm calling it a vegetable because the leaves are eaten as opposed to just being used as a flavoring. Easy to grow.

❀ Cool-season vegetable

❀ At least six hours' sun per day

❀ More information on page 142

❀ Extremely easy to grow from seeds. See my success on pages 46 to 47.

❀ Bush and vine types

❀ Warm-season vegetable

❀ At least six hours' sun per day

❀ More information on page 144

❀ Sometimes get pests, but none in my trials. Very easy.

❀ Cool-season vegetable

❀ Grows fastest in full sun, but tolerates some shade.

❀ More information on page 151

Many blue ribbon flowers are shown on pages 68 to 69 of this book. Or, for information on more flowers, see "Easy Container Gardens."

Greens, Mustard and Turnip

✿ Sometimes gets pests, but none in my trials. Very easy for us.

✿ Cool-season vegetable

✿ Grows fastest in full sun, but tolerates some shade.

✿ More information on page 155

Lettuce

✿ All the many varieties I tried did very well, but wilt a lot in too much heat or sun, even if the plant has just been watered. See profile on page 156 for solutions.

✿ Cool-season vegetable

✿ Grows fastest in full sun, but tolerates some shade.

Peppers

✿ Amazing! Highest producer of vegetables in my trials. All colors and varieties I tried thrived!

✿ Warm-season vegetable

✿ At least six hours' sun per day

✿ More information on page 160

Spinach

✿ One of the most nutritious vegetables. Easy. Looks rather non-descript alone but looks great with flowers.

✿ Cool-season vegetable

✿ Grows fastest in full sun, but tolerates some shade.

✿ More information on page 162

These Are Easy in Some Areas.

These four vegetables are extremely easy to grow in some but not all regions, so they rate a red ribbon. However, they require the same basic growing conditions as the ones on the previous page, which are:

❀ Use potting mix (not potting soil, top soil, or garden soil) with a brand name you trust.

❀ Use the fertilizer decribed on page 36.

❀ Be sure the pot has holes in the bottom (page 13).

❀ Don't bury the plant too deep (page 29).

❀ Plant in the right amount of light and in the correct season, which varies per plant. Check the individual plant profiles in the last chapter of this book for specifics.

❀ Water correctly (pages 38 to 40).

Cucumbers	Eggplant

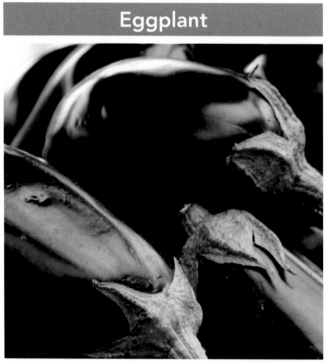

❀ Third most popular vegetable after tomatoes and peppers.

❀ Susceptible to downy mildew, which can be a real pain in the neck to control in some climates, particularly wet ones. Easy in other areas.

❀ Warm-season vegetable

❀ Full sun, at least six hours per day

❀ More information on page 152

❀ One of the easiest, warm-season vegetables to grow, provided you live in an area with 100 to 140 days of temperatures between 70 and 90 degrees.

❀ Looks great in a big pot alone, like a tropical plant.

❀ Warm-season vegetable

❀ Occasionally gets small holes in the leaves, which I ignore (see pages 42 to 43).

❀ Full sun, at least six hours per day

❀ More information on page 154

Okra

❀ One of the easiest vegetables in areas with warm temperatures for at least 50 to 60 days. Many cooler areas of the world will not produce good okra.

❀ I had great luck with it in my trials, giving it nothing but water after planting.

❀ One of the few, warm-season vegetables that looks good alone in a container (see page 53).

❀ Mainly used in soups and stews.

❀ Warm-season vegetable

❀ Full sun

❀ More information on page 158

Tomatoes

❀ Most popular vegetable in the US.

❀ Warm-season vegetable, but special cultivars are grown for areas with cooler temperatures, like the south Florida winters.

❀ Grown all over the country; easiest in places with at least a four month growing season and low humidity.

❀ I grew it successfully in high humidity without spraying, but I wasn't picky about leaf spot diseases. If a plant looked bad from a disease brought on by the humidity, I tossed it out and bought another. Overall, I was quite happy with my tomatoes.

❀ Full sun

❀ More information on page 164

Other Veggies That Made the Cut...

These seven vegetables are fairly easy to grow but not quite as easy or productive as the blue and red ribbon plants. They require the same basic growing conditions as the ones on the previous four pages.

Broccoli

✿ Timing is critical, can get cabbage worms, but quite popular nonetheless.

✿ Cool-season vegetable

✿ At least six hours' sun per day

✿ More information on page 146

Brussel Sprouts

✿ Ideal temperatures don't last long enough in most climates for large fruit, but many people are happy with small ones.

✿ Cool-season vegetable

✿ At least six hours' sun per day

✿ More information on page 147

Cabbage & Kale

✿ Frequently gets pests, but none in my trials. Quite popular.

✿ Cool-season vegetable

✿ At least six hours sun per day

✿ More information on page 148

Chard

✿ Easy to grow, but didn't look great in my trials.

✿ Cool-season vegetable

✿ At least four to eight hours' sun per day.

✿ More information on page 150.

Peas

✿ Easy, but didn't produce too many peas in my trials. Staking is a bit time consuming.

✿ Cool-season vegetable

✿ At least six hours' sun per day.

✿ More information on page 159.

Squash

✿ Very fast, worth growing, but gets quite a few pests.

✿ Warm-season vegetable.

✿ At least six hours' sun per day.

✿ More information on page 163.

Watermelon

✿ Very easy to grow, but only bore five fruit per container (with five vines)!

✿ Warm-season vegetable.

✿ At least six hours' sun per day.

✿ More information on page 166.

And The Ones That Didn't!

These vegetables are not emphasized in this book because they are unsuitable for containers or hard to grow. Some might do well in your area or when grown in the ground, so don't dismiss them entirely.

Artichokes

✿ Ideal conditions limited to mild regions of California; some gardeners enjoy smaller artichokes elsewhere.

✿ Cool-season vegetable

✿ At least six hours' sun per day

Asparagus

✿ A perennial (lasts more than one season) that isn't pretty in containers because the top is unwieldy.

✿ At least six hours' sun per day

Cantaloupe

✿ Did well planted in the ground, but not much fruit production in containers in my trials.

✿ Warm-season vegetable

✿ At least six hours' sun per day

Cauliflower

✿ Difficult to grow in many areas, but did ok in my trials.

✿ Cool-season vegetable

✿ At least six hours' sun per day.

Corn

✿ Plants grew but hardly produced any corn in my container trials. Need to grow quite a bit of corn together to insure pollination. Even then, corn is not a good container choice.

✿ Warm-season vegetable

✿ At least six hours' sun per day.

Pumpkins

✿ Fruit too large for containers.

✿ Cool-season vegetable

✿ At least six hours sun per day.

Root Veggies

✿ Root vegetables (carrots, potatoes, radishes, beets, onions etc) were not included in my container trials because the whole container has to be taken apart to harvest them.

Most Vegetables are Easier...

I had much more success in my vegetable trials than many of my neighbors who planted their vegetables in the ground. Potting mix (not potting soil, garden soil, or top soil) is almost always a superior, growing medium than the soil in your garden. Also, plants grown in container gardens attract fewer pests than those in the ground. Watering is harder, however, because containers dry out faster than the soil in your garden.

Only a few vegetables don't do as well in containers.

These Vegetables Don't Like Containers.

Asparagus isn't pretty in containers because the top is unwieldy.

Cantaloupe did well planted in the ground but didn't produce much fruit in my containers.

Corn grew decently but hardly produced any fruit in my containers. The corn it did produce was black!

Pumpkins are too large for containers.

In Containers than in the Ground.

Most Vegetables Did Extremely Well in Containers.

Luckily, most of my vegetables did well, <u>once I figured out the basics that you are learning in this chapter.</u> This hot pepper combo is an example. I did nothing to it after planting other than add water! And the production was quite high, as shown on the plates! Most of the peppers are hidden under the leaves.

Picked From This Pot (Right)
Shortly After Taking It's Photo

72 'Habanero' Peppers

34 'Jalapeno' Peppers

28 Chili Peppers

15 'Red Hot Cherry' Peppers

Know the Ultimate Size of Your Plants.

One of the biggest problems I had was underestimating the size of the vegetables I bought. I made many mistakes, particularly with warm-season vegetables, because they grew so much larger than I had ever imagined. To avoid the same mistakes, take this book with you to the garden center. Look up the vegetable you are considering in the index. All of the 18 vegetables I recommend for containers are included in the last chapter, with complete plant profiles. Look under "Average Size in a Container" and avoid my mistakes!

Nursery Tags Often Don't Indicate Mature Size.

Blooper!

What an awful looking arrangement! The large leaves growing on both sides are zucchini labeled as 'dwarf.' No size was given, so I assumed it would form a little vine that would cascade gently over the sides of this pot. Ha! It got HUGE and completely smothered the eggplant in back that was supposed to be the tall centerpiece!

Many nursery tags detail all sorts of valuable information about vegetables but neglect to tell you how large they get. Sometimes, you can guess how wide they grow if they specify how far apart to plant them. But, almost none I found said how tall they get.

This lack of information is made more difficult by the fact that most vegetables grow larger in the ground than in containers - and, the size also depends on the size of the container. So, be sure to take this book with you when you shop for vegetables. Look up the vegetable, or flower for that matter, in the index, and go to the page in the last chapter of this book that gives you the plant profile. Check under 'Average Size in a Container' for size information. This book doesn't have every vegetable in the world, not by a long shot, but at least it's a big help! And, it gives the size of every easy vegetable it lists.

Safe Bet: Plant Vegetables of Unknown Sizes Alone.

How big of a risk taker are you? I got burned so many times by underestimating the size of the vegetables that I ended up planting the unknowns in pots by themselves. That way, I could watch them for awhile to see if I needed to plant more plants in the same pot.

Then again, it depends sometimes on the cost of the plants. If you are paying fifty cents for a seedling, you don't have much to lose by sacrificing a few for a trial like mine!

I planted this 'Totem Tom' tomato (labeled as a small tomato ideal for containers) alone in this 14-inch wide container. Since I couldn't find any information about how large it got (I checked the label plus 20 online sources), I planned to let it grow for awhile before deciding to load up the pot with more plants. Waiting was a good choice because the small tomato completely filled this pot in no time. It produced about 25 great tomatoes - quite a few for such a small plant.

Important Point: Vegetables are Smaller in Containers.

And to make matters worse, I don't know how much smaller! But, I learned some generalities that will help you:

❀ The size of the vegetable plant is in direct proportion to the size of the pot.

❀ Most vegetables I tried did quite well planted in the side holes of side-planted baskets, but the plants grew to about 25 percent of normal size. The fruits were about 50 percent of normal size but tasted great!

❀ As a rule of thumb, vegetables planted in containers with diameters of 18 inches or larger grew to about 50 percent of normal size. Smaller containers yielded smaller plants. However, this is a guestimate based on my limited trials of about 221 containers.

These are cantaloupes planted in the side holes of this side-planted basket. The leaves got about 25 percent of the size of the ones I planted in the ground around it. The fruits were quite small as well. The vines grew all the way to the ground.

Cool-and Warm-Season Veggies

I made lots of mistakes by planting vegetables during the wrong season. Some need cool weather to bear fruit, while others have to have hot weather. Unfortunately, some garden centers sell them at the wrong time of year, so take this book with you when you buy plants to lessen any disappointments. Look up a vegetable profile in the last chapter and look under 'Hardiness' to find out it's temperature tolerances. Although each vegetable is classified by either warm or cool season, each one has it's own specific preferences which you will find in the last chapter.

Cool-Season Vegetables Generally Prefer 32 to 80 Degrees.

Broccoli

Brussels Sprouts

Cabbages

Chards

Collards

Greens

Lettuce

Peas

Spinach

Cool-season cabbage

Warm-Season Vegetables Prefer Temperatures Over 80 Degrees.

Beans

Cucumbers

Eggplants

Okra

Peppers

Squash

Tomatoes

Watermelons

Above, right: Warm-season eggplant
Opposite: This combination thrives in the cool season. Side-planted window box with juncus grass, mustard greens, pansies, and lettuce. See pages 78 to 89 for more information about side-planting.

For three-minute side-planting video, go to www.sideplanting.com.
Buying information for side-planted products on page 6.

Juncus Grass
1 plant from a 1-gallon pot
Plant Profile: Page 135

Mustard Greens
1 plant from a 1-gallon pot
Plant Profile: Page 155

'Matrix Blotch' Pansies
12 plants from 4" pots
Plant Profile: Page 137

'Mascara' Lettuce
9 plants from 4" pots
Plant Profile: Page 156

se Tolerate Some Shade...

the most common mistakes is growing sun vegetables in too much You see sun on your patio at noon and assume that it's a sunny spot. what about the rest of the day? If the sun starts shining on your patio at 11 a.m. and stops at 1 p.m., that it's two hours of sun per day, not enough for any vegetable! Look at your garden many times so that you can see what time the sun starts shining on it and what time it's done. That will tell you how many hours of sun you truly have.

And to make matters more complicated, the sun moves throughout the year. Your summer vegetable spot could turn shady in the winter or vice versa. So, be sure you check your seasonal light conditions in locations where you want to grow vegetables.

Prefer Full Sun, but Live On as Little as Four to Five Hours per Day

Arugula
Plant Profile: Page 142

Chard
Plant Profile: Page 150

Collard Greens
Plant Profile: Page 151

Lettuce
Plant Profile: Page 156

Spinach
Plant Profile: Page 162

While These Need Full Sun.

Need Full Sun, For at Least Six Hours Per Day (Preferably Longer).

Beans
Plant Profile: Page 144

Broccoli
Plant Profile: Page 146

Brussels Sprouts
Plant Profile: Page 147

Cabbage and Kale
Plant Profile: Page 148

Cucumber
Plant Profile: Page 152

Eggplant
Plant Profile: Page 154

Okra
Plant Profile: Page 158

Peas
Plant Profile: Page 159

Peppers
Plant Profile: Page 160

Squash and Zucchini
Plant Profile: Page 163

Tomatoes
Plant Profile: Page 164

Watermelon
Plant Profile: Page 166

How Many Veggies Does One Pot Produce?

Vegetable production varies considerably, based on type of vegetable and container size. For example, I planted many different types of peppers in side-planted containers. The 'Habenero' produced more than any of the other peppers. Had I known ahead of time that four plants would produce 236 peppers, I might have planted just one plant! Learn what you can about how much one plant will produce (shown throughout this book) so you don't plant more than you and all your friends can eat!

Our Record: 236 Habenero Peppers from One Container (Right)

I picked 236 peppers all at once from this container on a column (shown right) - when it was close to the end of the season. Had I been picking frequently, my overall harvest would have been even larger!

This container (shown right, buying info page 6) includes four 'Habanero' pepper plants located in the top of a side-planted container.

I planted the basket in June, and it lasted until mid-October with no care at all other than water!

Watermelon Only Bore Five Fruit.

Growing watermelon in containers might not be worth it, but it sure was a conversation piece! Visitors were amazed at the little watermelons sitting in the hot sun on the driveway.

As is the case with most container gardens, the watermelons didn't grow as large as they would have in the ground, only about one-third the size.

I made the mistake of picking them at the wrong time (see pages 55 to 56 for more info). But, the plant was so easy to grow, it was definitely worth the trouble.

For three-minute, side-planting and column installation instructions for the products shown right, see the videos at www.sideplanting.com.

1ST

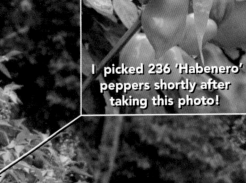
I picked 236 'Habenero' peppers shortly after taking this photo!

Angelonia
(2 plants from 4" pots)
Plant profile: Page 130

Rust Coleus
(8 plants from 4" pots)
Plant profile: Page 132

'Golden Variegated' Sage
(8 plants from 4" pots)
Plant profile: Page 138

'Dark Star' Coleus
(8 plants from 4" pots)
Plant profile: Page 132

'Habenero' Pepper
(4 plants from 4" pots)
Plant profile: Page 160

Best Containers for Vegetables

Use the Largest Containers You Can Afford with Warm-Season Veggies!

I frequently planted vegetables in containers that were too small. This is particularly easy to do with the warm-season vegetables, which generally grow larger than the cool-season ones. They look so small in their little pots at the garden center! Considering the fact that I planted 221 containers and <u>never</u> planted vegetables in one that was too large, I have learned an important lesson!

I have included the ideal container size with each vegetable profile in the last chapter of this book.

Some advantages of large containers:

❁ Vegetables grow larger and produce more fruit.

❁ Plants last longer because their roots have more space to grow.

❁ More water can be stored, so you don't have to water as often.

❁ Many vegetables look much better. Peppers, for example, look quite leggy in containers that are too small.

I call this the 'Rolls Royce Garden' because the containers are not only huge - one a full four feet tall - but also expensive! If you have a low budget, try my $5 ideas! The containers are from www.potterylandusa.com (or, in the greater Atlanta area, at JAM'n Designs, 16 Forest Parkway, Forest Park, Georgia, Sheds 34 E, F, & G , Atlanta state Farmers Market, 404-234-0453).

Budget Idea: $5 Large Containers

I found inexpensive, large containers in a surprising location - the party section of large, retail stores. They are called 'party tubs' and are designed to hold ice. I drilled holes in the bottom and planted quite a few of them (instructions shown, opposite).

These plastic containers (19"L x 16"W x 9"D) come in a wide range of bright colors. To support vining plants, I bought $8 wooden trellises and sprayed them bright colors with outdoor spray paint. After drilling some small holes in the back of the plastic pots, I used twist ties to attach the trellises to the containers, so they wouldn't fall over. Once the trellises were attached, I added soil to stabilize them further. See Chapter 4 for the results.

Ornamental cabbages planted with dusty miller and edible violas in a $5 container.

Be Sure the Container Has a Hole in the Bottom.

If the container doesn't have a hole in the bottom, the vegetables will drown and die (unless the container is specifically designed for self watering). Many containers come with holes. If yours doesn't, take it to the local home improvement store (if you can lift it), and ask the salesman what kind of drill bit you need to drill a 3/4 inch diameter hole.

Plastic pots are fairly easy to drill through. Ceramic, terra cotta, or clay are harder. You need a hammer drill (essential!) for these hard materials, and it can take quite a while to drill a hole through a hard, thick pot. Choose the correct drill bit from your home improvement store. Turn the pot upside down, and place it on a towel (if the edge might chip). Drill for short periods (about 15 seconds) and stop, so the drill can cool off. Then, drill again, and keep going for short periods until the hole is done. Yes, I have broken some, but not many. Protective eye-wear is a good idea to prevent eye damage from flying chips.

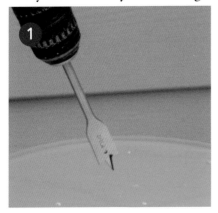

Drill bit I used to drill holes in plastic pots. Always ask the salesman at the home improvement store which bit to use on the different container materials.

After placing the pot upside down on a table (or any safe, stable surface), the hole is easily drilled through plastic. I left the price tag on the bottom to keep the plastic from splitting. Use masking tape if the tag isn't in the center.

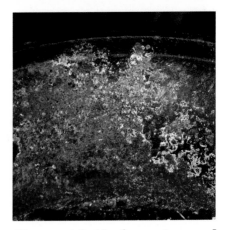

This 3/4 inch hole is plenty large enough for this container, which is 16 inches wide. Some containers come with multiple holes, which is fine. Just be sure the water can drain out!

Container Materials Didn't Matter, except for Metal.

Aluminum does not rust. This pot has been outside for six years.

All of the container materials I used performed equally as well, except for metal. Many of the metal pots on the market now are meant for indoor use and quickly rust outdoors. Aluminum doesn't rust, but most metal containers are made of iron, which does rust, or brass, which oxidizes and eventually turns black. I bought a beautiful, black, cast iron pot, and it started rusting within a week! Some iron containers are meant to rust, but many other types of metal are not.

The rusted finish of a cast iron pot I bought, not knowing that it would rust.

Vegetables are Easier in Larger Pots.

Okra is a large plant that thrived in this large, cobalt blue container. It grew larger, produced more fruit, and required less water because of the large pot size. The okra plant is loaded with fruit, which are covered up by the leaves. <u>For more detailed okra information, see page 158.</u>

The fruit really hides behind the leaves, so much so that I didn't see it when it should have been harvested! Okra grows slowly in cooler weather but speeds up when it gets hot, so be sure to look for the fruit frequently. You can pick them when they are at their best - four to six inches long.

The flowers and other ornamental plants added more than just beauty. They extended the life of the whole container garden by three months. The okra and petunias died when they were three months old. Once the dead plants were cut off, the others lasted for an additional three months.

Once the okra died, I just cut the dead branches off, and the rest of the plants looked great for another three months.

Cultural Information

Light: Full sun, at least six hours per day

Season: Okra is one of the easiest vegetables for areas that have warm temperatures for at least 50 to 60 days. Many cooler areas of the world will not produce good okra. Okra prefers days of 85 degrees or warmer and nights at least in the 60's. The rest of the plants thrive in temperatures from 40 to 95 degrees.

Lifespan: The okra and petunias lasted about three months. The other plants kept going for an additional three months after the okra died.

Care: Fertilize on planting day with a slow-release mix described on page 36. Repeat if the leaves look yellowish or washed-out, although the fertilizer should last from six to nine months.

Trim the sweet potato vine as needed.

Water: Water thoroughly, if the plants show signs of wilt or the soil feels dry when you push your fingertip into the potting mix (see pages 38 to 40). I watered this one every day in mid summer (after it was about a month old) and every other day in cooler weather.

Troubleshooting: I missed the first harvest! Since the okra fruit were hidden by the leaves, I didn't see them when they were they ready to pick, about four to six inches long. It's as if they appeared overnight and grew as big as bananas! I also had a few holes in the leaves of the sweet potato, which I ignored.

Planting Plan: Easy. Simply plant the okra against the back of the pot, centering it with the sides. Tuck the other plants along the edges. Be sure to plant in good-quality potting <u>mix</u>, not garden soil, top soil, or potting soil, which can kill your plants. Other important planting tips are shown on pages 32 to 35.

Container: Anamese's *Tall Milan* in blue (36.5"H x 15.5"W). Shop for it at www.anamese.com.

Additional Comments: I don't replace all the potting mix in a container this size each time I replant in it - only about the top 18 inches. Don't try styrofoam pellets in the bottom - they are biodegradable and disintegrate after the first watering!

Best Time to Pick: Pick okra when four to six inches long.

Okra
One plant from a 5" pot
Plant Profile: Page 158

Coleus 'Kong Scarlet'
Two plants from 6" pots
Plant Profile: Page 132

'Blackie' Sweet Potato
Two plants from 4" pots
Plant Profile: Page 140

Lime Sweet Potato
Two plants from 4" pots
Plant Profile: Page 140

'Blanket' Petunia
One plant from a 4" pot
Plant Profile: Page 137

Plant Closer Together in Containers...

Space Container Plants Closer than Those Planted in the Ground.

Container gardens are planted much closer than gardens in the ground if you are using vegetables that are somewhat mature, like these ornamental cabbages. This technique was quite difficult for me to get used to when I first started container gardening. My background in landscape architecture had taught me to leave quite a bit of space around plants, so their roots had room in which to spread. (This wide spacing is important for permanent plantings because roots of long-lived plantings need space to support the growing plants above ground.)

Container gardens are temporary, with most people using them for decorative, short-lived displays (four to six months). Since most people want quick results, plant as close as you can in your containers. And, yes, they live and flourish! One mantra of experienced container gardeners is "Jam them in!" which is easy once you get the hang of it.

The only time to vary this practice is when, on planting day, your centerpiece vegetable is actually shorter than the surrounding flowers. Although the centerpiece is the tallest plant in the arrangement, it is often difficult to find larger sizes in garden centers. For example, you want to plant an eggplant that will grow four feet tall, and surround it by begonias, that will grow to eight inches tall. The largest eggplant you can find at your garden center is five inches tall, and the begonias are larger. Plant the eggplant first, alone in the pot. Give it a few weeks until it is double the flower height, and then add the flowers around it. This practice keeps the flowers from smothering the eggplant. See the pages 34 to 36 for examples.

I took this photo right after planting this container with ornamental cabbages and violas. It should last four to six months.

Planting a Bowl

To remove a plant from the pot, turn the pot upside down over your hand, and let it drop. If it doesn't come out easily, squeeze the sides of the pot together. Once the plant is removed, loosen the roots if they are growing in a circle around the edge of the root ball.

Dip the root ball in a bucket of water to make it easier to fit into the desired spot. Wet roots have the consistency of modeling clay and are easier to mold and reduce when wet.

Place the cabbage along the back edge of the pot, with the top of the root ball a little lower than the edge of the pot. Since this bowl is so low, no potting mix is needed in the bottom of the pot, or the cabbage would have been too tall to fit.

Add potting mix around the center plant, so the tops of the smaller, edge plants will be at the same level as the centerpiece. One of the easiest ways to kill plants (except tomatoes) is piling potting mix around the stems of a plant, which quickly rots it. Better to plant slightly above the grade rather than below it.

After wetting the roots of the edge plants, place them as close as you can in front of and along the sides of the cabbage. Angle them out a bit, so they look pretty along the edge of the pot. I fit 16 violas in this small pot. They came out of an 18-pack, which is considerably cheaper than single pots.

After planting the edge plants, fertilize with the product described on page 36. Place the fertilizer on the potting mix, not on top of the plants. However, if you mess up, the fertilizer will not burn the plants. Use the amount shown on the label for the size pot you are planting.

Plant Tiny Vegetable Plants First...

Many large vegetables, like tomatoes, peppers, and eggplant, are tiny when you purchase them, only about 10 percent of their mature size. Flowers, on the other hand, are often sold at 50 to 75 percent of their mature size. If you plant them in the same pot at the same time, the flowers will overrun the vegetables. Plant the vegetables first, as shown below, and let them grow larger than the smaller, edge plants before planting the smaller ones.

I picked nine, huge eggplants from this plant shortly after taking this photo (shown, right). They weighed 20 pounds! This container combo required no care other than water after I planted it correctly. <u>For more detailed eggplant information, see page 154.</u>

This is the size of the eggplant when I first planted it. I waited until it was larger to add the flowers.

Eggplants come in a wide variety of shapes, sizes, and colors.

This eggplant was quite small when I bought it (left). So small, in fact, that I was worried that planting flowers near it wouldn't work because the flowers would swallow up the small eggplant.

So, I planted the eggplant (left, just after planting) and waited about two weeks for it to reach 24 inches tall. The eggplant grew really quickly because the weather was hot. Then, I surrounded it with yellow flowers (melampodium).

This technique worked beautifully. After the flowers were planted, I did nothing at all other than water and stake the eggplant branches that started to fall.

Here are some other key facts about this really easy combo:

✿ This one eggplant produced an amazing 20 pounds of fruit! I only harvested once, which was a mistake because frequent picking increases vegetable production. But, I was thrilled with what I got from this one plant that was so little trouble to grow.

✿ The eggplants were huge! The largest one measured a full ten inches long!

✿ The container is huge, which encouraged the plant to grow large enough to produce such large fruit. Eggplant planted in a smaller container would produce smaller fruit.

✿ I only planted three, large melampodium plants in front of the eggplant to give it more room to grow. Because both the eggplant and melampodium were large, the container looked full on planting day.

✿ The container is in full sun. Remember that most vegetables require at least six hours of sun each day.

And Add Flowers Later.

Eggplant
1 plant from a 5" pot
Plant Profile: Page 154

Melampodium
3 plants from 6" pots
Plant Profile: Page 136

Fertilizer: Organic vs. Chemical

Vegetables need a lot of fertilizer. I found one that had everything they needed, and I only had to apply once! It didn't burn any of the plants or stain any patios, either! And it's won environmental awards!

Fertilizer I Used on All the Plants in this Book

Fertilizer is one of the most important components of blue ribbon plants and easy container gardens. Remember, the blue ribbon plants only require water after you plant them. But, that is possible <u>only</u> if you use a fertilizer at planting time that lasts the entire lifespan of the arrangement. Without fertilizer, the plants will slowly turn yellow and decline.

I have only found one fertilizer that works perfectly every time on both flowers and vegetables. And, it is forgiving. If you use too much, it doesn't burn the plants. It is also excellent for the environment, winning the 2005 Gulf Guardian Award from the EPA Gulf of Mexico Program Partnership.

This fertilizer is slow-release, meaning its little pellets release the nutrients over a period of time. It is a great improvement over the liquids you apply weekly with a hose sprayer! However, there are many slow-release products on the market. I have tested every one I could get my hands on, and none come close to this one. Some either don't last as long or don't have all the nutrients plants need. Others release all their nutrients at once if there is a lot of rain, burning the plants.

This fertilizer lasts nine months in 'average' conditions. If you see the plants yellowing a bit, just add some more. Sprinkle it on top of the potting mix, following the instructions on the label.

Many potting mixes also include fertilizer. I haven't found one yet that lasts long, so I add this one at planting time as well. This fertilizer is available at www.kinsmangarden.com.

Look for These Ingredients on the Label.

As I told you on page 10, I have killed many plants with the wrong fertilizer. I have also been through fertilizers that simply didn't make the grade. They included some but not all of the elements a plant needs. Weird, hard-to-diagnose, nutritional deficiencies developed that were time consuming, annoying, and definitely not easy.

Plants are like people - they need lots of different nutrients to keep them alive. If you have a vitamin deficiency, you might get quite sick. Same thing with a plant. Learn to read the fertilizer label to make sure it includes *all* the nutrients your plants need.

Most fertilizers include nitrogen, phosphorus (phosphate), and potassium (potash). But most, including some of the best-selling brands, don't include the micronutrients that plants need. *So look for boron, copper, iron, manganese, and magnesium as well. Do not buy a product that doesn't include these micronutrients, or your plants could suffer later.*

Vegetables require quite a few nutrients to grow well. I searched for the product that would provide those nutrients with the least time and risk. The product (shown, left) worked beautifully.

Differences between Chemical and Organic Fertilizers

✿ Chemical fertilizers may include any and all nutrients a plant needs to grow. Organic fertilizers either have primarily only one element or more that are at very low levels.

✿ Organic fertilizers are usually slow-release, which is good. However, they take quite a while to work. The idea behind organics is to slowly improve the structure of the soil, not provide quick nutrients. So, if your plants need nutrients quickly, like annuals or vegetables in container gardens, I recommend the chemical fertilizer shown on the previous page. It has both slow- and fast-acting elements, and it includes all 16 elements your plants need to grow. Plus, it isn't an environmental threat.

✿ Organic fertilizers, like manure, are free from many sources. All chemical fertilizers cost money.

✿ Organic fertilizers are quite varied. Some are really mild, and others, like Milorganite, can burn plants. I heard it repelled deer, so I poured in around the edge of a bed and lost all the plants near the edge!

✿ The long term effects of organics are excellent, in that they can greatly diminish the amount of chemicals needed in your yard. They are more useful in a garden situation, where they add to the soil over a period of years, than in a container situation.

✿ Learn about any organic fertilizer prior to using it, so that you understand specific risks and benefits. Go to www.cdcg.org/goOrganic.html for more info.

Watering Basics

Watering takes the most time of any container garden chore, and vegetables need quite a bit of water. Plants in containers need more water than plants in the ground because their root systems are smaller, and the roots are where plants store most of their water. The root system of a plant in the ground is three times the diameter of the plant. Not so for container plants - the roots are only as large as the container.

I was pleasantly surprised by the watering needs of side-planted containers. Prior to using them, I was concerned that the coco fiber liner would not hold water for long. I pictured myself permanently standing next to a container pouring water on it! Luckily, that was not the case. Read these two pages to learn quickly what it took me hundreds of trials to master.

Water with a Gentle Stream.

Check out the nozzle on the watering wand shown above. This nozzle diffuses the water, so you don't blow the little plants right out of the pots. The same effect comes from a nozzle that fits directly on the hose. I like the hose nozzles that have a lot of different settings, so I can use a gentle stream for soaking a container or a strong stream for cleaning a patio.

Factors That Affect Water Use

Peppers require more water than some other vegetables, like okra.

- ❀ **Sun or shade.** Plants use one-third to one-half as much water in shade than in full sun.

- ❀ **Temperature.** Plants use more water when the temperatures are high.

- ❀ **Wind.** Plants in windy areas require more water than plants in calm areas.

- ❀ **Reflections from walls.** If you have a light-colored wall facing south with no shade, you may have to plant succulents to take the reflected heat if you live in a very hot climate.

- ❀ **Soil.** Good-quality potting mix usually includes peat moss, which holds water better than cheaper, sandy soils.

- ❀ **Plant type.** Plant species vary in their need for water. Peppers (left), for example, need more water than okra.

- ❀ **Container size.** Large containers with small plants require much less water than small containers filled to the brim with large plants.

- ❀ **How long the plant has been in the container.** As plants age in containers, their roots fill the pot, leaving less space for water.

How to Tell When a Plant Needs Water

Water when you see signs of wilt or if the soil feels dry to the touch. Use your finger to test the soil. Push it into the soil about an inch or so. Low-water plants, like cacti and succulents, need less water and can go longer with dry soil.

Knowing when to water is very important because many container plants die from overwatering. If the plant looks wilted and the potting mix has been wet for several days, the plant is drowning and will probably die. It may have root rot. You might try a fungicide if the plant is very important to you. The exception to this rule is lettuce. It often wilts when the potting mix is soaked, often as a response to heat or sunlight. Leave it alone, and it will recover quickly. But, be sure to check the potting mix to be sure it is well hydrated.

How Much Water to Apply

Water thoroughly with each application. The biggest watering mistake people make is to give the plant just a little bit of water. Typically in this case that is the same as giving a person dying of thirst just a teaspoonful of water! Soak the plant thoroughly until you see a steady stream of water coming out of the bottom of the pot. A slow soaking is better than a fast hit with the hose because it allows the roots time to absorb the water.

Re-Hydrating Really Dry Plants

Plants in a severe state of wilt that look like they are near death may benefit from a bottom-soaking. The soil is dry and has shrunk away from the sides of the pot, and when you water from the top, the water just washes down between the sides of the pot and the soil. In addition, the soil feels hard, like a chunk of wood, and isn't absorbing the water. If this is the case, put the whole pot on top of a container of water - a saucer or baking pan is ideal. Leave it overnight. The water will be absorbed by the soil like a sponge, and your plant will probably be quite healthy in the morning!

Water Needs Change as a Plant Ages

Plants need a lot of water right after they are planted. Then, as the roots grow, water requirements lessen. Once the roots fill the pot, the plant needs more water again!

Watering Shortcuts

Automatic Drip Systems

<u>This is the best idea I have for easy container gardens. Install an automatic system with a timer, and never drag a hose around again! I will not go through another summer without one!</u>

Drip irrigation hooks up to your hose or sprinkler system and has an emitter for each pot. Systems are easily available in kit form and fairly easy to install, or your sprinkler repairman can install them for you. These systems greatly reduce the time spent watering but do require some maintenance because the emitters can fall out of the pots or become clogged. There are many different types of emitters available, so be sure yours fit the size of your pots. Some emitters are designed for very small pots, for example, and will not deliver enough water to a large container. Drip systems are designed to water a lot of pots at once, which can be a disadvantage, if only one plant needs it and the others don't.

Water-Holding Polymers

Many companies are developing water-holding gels (like Terrasorb or Hortasorb) to hold water in containers longer. These materials look like rock salt when they are dry. They absorb water and expand into a jello-like substance when soaked in water. A tablespoon of polymer expands to about a quart of wet material. It is added to the potting soil before planting. Desire Foard, owner of Gardenstyle and creator of the beautiful container gardens along the streets in Naples, Florida, uses these materials in most of her containers. They cut her watering chores down by about one-third. She saturates the material in water for 10 to 15 minutes before adding it to the potting soil. It is very important to wet it before you add it to the soil. One lady told me all her plants died after she tried the polymers. My guess is that she either added it dry or added too much. Be sure to follow the instructions to the letter on the box.

Many potting mixes now include water-holding polymers. All the potting mixes I use include them (except the mixes I use for succulents), and I have had excellent luck with them. The brands I have tried cut watering down by about one-third.

I have heard reports of potting mixes with water-holding polymers that retain too much water, causing the plants to rot. I haven't yet had any negative results with these mixes, and have tried them both in dry and wet years.

Large Pots

Large pots hold more potting mix than smaller ones, so they require less water. This pot is a full 30 inches tall. I have had it for years planted with the canna lilies you see here. I have gone for weeks on end without watering it at all! I leave the cannas in all year. They die back in the winter and reappear the following spring in Georgia (zone seven). I never water them at all in the winter.

When I add edge plants that require more water, like these lime green sweet potato plants, I water more, about twice a week. Smaller pots filled with sweet potato plants in the same place would require water every day!

Vegetable Supports, Jiffy Pots

Support Anything that Falls Over.

Left to right: A loose tie around a single stake, obelisk, and trellis

Many vegetables need some sort of support to keep them from falling over. I use small, green stakes for smaller branches, like peppers. For larger vegetables that do not stand up on their own, I use either trellises or obelisks. Vining vegetables, like cucumbers, do best with trellises while bushy vegetables, like bush tomatoes, do best with obelisks. Choose attractive hardware to keep the container garden looking its best.

Be sure to use loose ties to keep the vegetables attached to the support. Tight ties will eventually cut into the branch, killing it.

Working with Jiffy Pots

1. Keep the Jiffy pots very moist until they are planted in the ground. Once they dry out, it is tricky to get them wet again. If this happens, it is easiest to put a few inches of water in a pan and put the peat pots in it to absorb water from below. Leave them in the water for at least four hours.

2. Cut the plastic off the rim with scissors.

3. Tear or cut away the remaining peat rim of the pot, so none of it is left exposed above the ground.

4. Tear or cut away the bottom half of the pot before planting it. Sometimes, it just falls off. Don't try for perfection here! If all the pot falls away comes off, it doesn't matter.

5. Plant the pot so the top is even or a little above the ground. Except for tomatoes, don't plant too deeply or plants could rot.

6. Water thoroughly.

See www.bonnieplants.com for a short video demonstration.

Pest Control: Most Veggies Attract...

Inspect Plants Often.

Vegetables frequently get pests, more so than annual flowers or landscape plants. If you want to plant vegetables with the least chance of getting pests, see the blue and red ribbon choices on pages 14 to 17.

Be sure to inspect your plants often. Pests can devastate vegetables quickly. Many times, they are easy to control if you treat them early.

More Bugs: To Spray or Not to Spray?

For years, I have worked on testing flowers to find out which ones give the highest performance with the least amount of care. Luckily, I have found many that seldom attract pests. These flowers are designated with blue ribbons, which is explained on pages 68 to 69 in this book. For more blue ribbon flowers, see the companion book, "Easy Container Gardens."

Not so for vegetables. Most attract many more bugs than my favorite flowers. For specifics, see the plant profiles in the last chapter of this book.

I didn't spray my vegetable plants unless I thought the bugs would significantly hurt them. Eggplant (left), for example, had tiny holes in the leaves, which I ignored. All of the holey eggplant bore tons of fruit!

This container features 'Ichiban' eggplant surrounded by sweet potato vine. Purple petunias, angelonia, and 'Gold Mound' duranta are planted in the ground around it. The container is from www.potterylandusa.com or www.jamndesigns.com in the greater Atlanta area.

The 'Ichiban' eggplant is meant to be a slender fruit. The plant is not as attractive as some other eggplants, but 'Ichiban' bears a ton of fruit!

More Bugs than Flowers Do.

Downy Mildew, My Nemesis

1 and 2: Leaves that show evidence of downy mildew. 3: Be sure to cut off affected leaves before spraying the rest of the plant. 4: Spray both the tops and bottoms of the leaves. If you don't spray the bottoms, the plant could die.

Downy mildew was far and above the worst pest I had in my trials. It showed up on all of my squash (including zucchini) and cucumbers starting in July. It was one of the wettest years in history, which made the mildew problem a lot worse than it normally is.

This pest will kill the plants unless you spray like clockwork, once a week. Here are some facts:

❁ Downy mildew isn't appearing in all parts of the country, but there is plenty in Georgia! It is worse in rainy years.

❁ Cut off infected leaves prior to spraying.

❁ If you don't spray every week religiously, it won't work.

❁ You have to spray both the tops and bottoms of the leaves. This can be tricky, but give it your best shot.

❁ Look for varieties that are resistant to this nasty pest.

❁ Clean your scissors or trimmers after using them to discourage the spread of downy mildew.

General Spraying Tips

❁ Don't spray for a few tiny holes. Wait, and see if the pest problem is worth the trouble of spraying.

❁ Take a leaf to a local garden center, and ask them for the least toxic spray for whatever is eating it. Be sure they understand that it is for vegetables, so you don't poison the fruit. Many sprays are dangerous to use with something you plan to eat.

❁ Get the name of the spray, and research it online. Google 'problems with' and then the name of the spray so you can understand the risks.

❁ Understand that 'organic' does not mean safe. Arsenic is organic. See page 37 for information about organic fertilizer.

❁ Follow the instructions on the label to the letter. <u>My assistant was hospitalized following exposure to a common pesticide, which shows how easy it is for accidents to occur with these substances.</u>

Harvest at the Right Time and...

Pick Vegetables When They are the Best Size to Eat.

Each vegetable tastes best when it is picked at a particular size, usually when it is young and tender. Okra, for example, tastes best when picked at four to six inches in length. Yellow squash tastes best before the warts have started to form. Since these vegetables hide under the leaves and grow quickly, inspect plants often. The last chapter of this book tells you the optimum harvest size for each vegetable.

Many Vegetables Hide Under the Leaves.

Dwarf Peppers

I missed harvesting some vegetables because I never saw them! Many hide under the leaves, so be sure to check frequently. You don't want to miss them.

Can you see the peppers in the container shown left? Dwarf peppers are planted behind the purple angelonia flowers shown on the top of this basket on a column. About 20 peppers were present when this photo was taken.

They are easier to see in the close up below. I moved the flowers aside to take the photo. Like many peppers, they change color from green to red.

Baskets and columns from Kinsman Company (www.kinsmangarden.com). Large pots from Tom Oswald (www.jamndesigns.com) and Pottery Land (www.potterylandusa.com).

For three-minute planting and column installation instructions, see the videos at www.sideplanting.com. Buying information on page six.

Look for Veggies That are Hiding!

Cucumbers

Zucchini

Dwarf Peppers

Dwarf Tomatoes

Growing Beans from Seeds

Most of the vegetables I planted were garden center plants, not seeds. Since this book is about easy container gardening, it follows that buying plants is much easier than spending the time growing seeds. However, I couldn't find bean plants, so I decided to try seeds (after I had heard that they were easy!) For more detailed bean information, see page 144.

Bean seeds are large and fast-growing, but many other vegetable seeds are quite a bit more difficult. These bush beans were one of the easiest and most fun vegetables I grew. Both the flowers and the beans are purple and white. Most of the flowers and beans stayed hidden under the leaves, but enough showed to make an interesting display.

And, talk about easy! All I did was plant few a seeds and left them alone! They germinated in just a few days. I put an attractive, wrought iron trellis over them because they started to fall over, but other than that, didn't touch them other than to water.

Top: Place seeds on top of soil and plant them about one inch down. Bottom: They sprouted a few days later!

Cultural Information

Light: Full sun, at least six hours per day

Season: Plant when the temperatures are warm. Start seeds when temperatures are above 55 degrees. They won't germinate in cooler temperatures. More climate information on page 144.

Lifespan: About three months

Days to Harvest: 50 to 60 from seed. I didn't find these beans at garden centers already germinated, so I don't know how long it takes to harvest if you buy plants instead of seeds.

Care: Fertilize on planting day with a slow-release mix described on page 36.

Water: Water thoroughly if the plants show signs of wilt, or the soil feels dry when you push your fingertip into the potting mix (see pages 38 to 40). I watered this one every day.

Troubleshooting: Some holes in the leaves, but the beans didn't seem to mind. Birds are often attracted to beans. If your birds start eating your beans, put some netting over them.

Planting Plan: I planted a total of eight seeds in this pot, which has an inner diameter of 18 inches. Plant about one inch deep. Once they germinated, I cut off about one-third of the weakest ones at the ground. Be sure to plant in good-quality potting mix, not garden soil, top soil, or potting soil, which can kill your plants. Other important planting tips are shown on pages 32 to 35.

Container: Although I'm generally not a fan of plastic pots, this one is an example of some of the newer plastics that actually look good. 18-inch inner diameter.

Harvesting: Pick beans when they are still thin, and you can't see the seeds sticking out. If you wait too long, go ahead and cook them. They might not be as tender, but will still taste good. Don't pick them when they are wet. Pick frequently to encourage more flowers and beans (more on harvesting on page 144).

Notes: The seeds came from www.reneesgarden.com. They are labeled 'Tricolor Bush Beans' in gold, purple, and green. The seeds match the color of the beans (not exactly, but almost!). I planted the gold (which looked white to me) and the purple, but not the green.

1ST

Look under the leaves on the left side, and you will see about 60 white beans. Plant Profile: Page 144

Look under the leaves on the right side, and you will see about 50 purple beans. Plant Profile: Page 144

Take This Book with You...

Four Important Facts to Know <u>Before</u> Buying a Vegetable

Take this book with you when you go to garden centers. When you see a plant you are considering buying, check the index to find the appropriate pages.

How many plants have you killed in your lifetime? Many of these fatalities could have been avoided if you knew key facts about the plants BEFORE you bought them. This is especially true with vegetables, not only because they are trickier to grow than many other plants, but also because their labels sometimes lack key information. Here is the basic information you need:

1. <u>Is this vegetable easy to grow in containers?</u> If you are a beginner or a serial plant killer, you shouldn't be attempting to grow difficult plants! Even if you are an experienced gardener, some vegetables don't do well in containers. Just check in the index, look up the plant, and the information is easy to find!

2. <u>When does it grow in your area?</u> Many gardeners plant vegetables at the wrong time of year. The last chapter of this book tells you when to plant all 18 vegetables that I recommend for containers. You might need to check with your county extension for a few, but all of the vegetable profiles include the temperature requirements for each vegetable. Just look under 'Hardiness' in each vegetable profile in the last chapter of this book.

3. <u>How much fruit will it produce?</u> Since one of my containers produced 236 peppers (from four plants), I learned to figure that our ahead of time what to expect! I would have only planted one pepper plant had I known! Find this information under 'Production' in each vegetable profile in the last chapter of this book.

4. <u>What size does it grow in a container?</u> The little plants look so cute in the tiny, garden center pots! It's hard to believe how HUGE many of them will grow. You need to know this information so that you can choose the right containers and arrange the plants properly in their containers. In each vegetable profile in the last chapter of this book, look under "Average Size in a Container" for this information. I didn't test every single variety (there are 25,000 varieties of tomatoes!) but at least you will know quite a bit more from seeing how large many tomatoes grow than you knew before.

Some Garden Centers Have Plants That Don't Fit Your Season.

Blooper!

These gorgeous cabbages were planted at the wrong time of year. They turned ugly quickly and had to be thrown away.

I purchased cabbage in spring (April) in a garden center in Georgia. I didn't know that cabbages grow in cool weather and go into a decline in temperatures above 80 to 85 degrees. These temperatures are ideal for spring in many locations of the country - areas where the temperatures stay cool for a few months, giving the cool-season vegetables time to mature in cool weather.

Not so for Georgia, where the temperatures can hit the 90's in early June. <u>But, the label didn't say anything about the ideal temperatures for these plants.</u>

About a month after planting, I had to completely take apart this basket to get the awful, bug-infested cabbages out of it. Take this book with you and look up each vegetable to avoid this experience. Temperature requirements are clearly stated for each vegetable in the profiles in the last chapter of this book. Check the index for page numbers.

To the Garden Center.

Know the Size of the Plant Before Buying It.

Blooper!

The Brussels sprouts are the cute, little plants with the silver-grey leaves planted in the side holes of this basket on a column (left). I thought they would be perfect as side plants because they looked a little like the cabbage that had done well for me in this situation before. Was I ever wrong! Brussels sprouts grow tall to allow the sprouts along the stem have to have room to grow. They work well as a centerpiece but are too large for the side holes. I ended up having to completely take apart this basket in order to replace them. The plant tag said nothing whatsoever about how tall they get!

To find out the sizes of each vegetable in a container, check out the last chapter of this book. Each vegetable profile includes a section called "Average Size in a Container." I didn't test every single variety (there are 25,000 varieties of tomatoes!) but at least you will know quite a bit more from seeing how large many tomatoes grow than you knew before.

Left: The silver-leafed Brussels sprouts had to be thrown away because they were much too big for the sides of this basket. Has I had this book with me, I simply could have looked up Brussel sprouts in the last chapter and found their size under "Average Size in a Container." Under "Use," it also clearly states that Brussel sprouts don't do well planted in the size holes of side-planted baskets! For information on the basket and border column, see pages 78 to 85. Buying information on page six.

Know How Easy a Plant is Prior to Buying It.

Some vegetables, like bell peppers, are very easy to grow. Others, like cauliflower, are a bit tricky. If you have this book with you in the garden center, you can find out how difficult a vegetable is to grow prior to buying it.

Just look in the index, find the page numbers for the vegetable you are considering buying, and skim the pages. This simple practice could save you a ton of time, frustration, and money!

Left: Cauliflower can be difficult to grow.

Right: Peppers are quite easy to grow.

Chapter 2

Creating Attractive Combos

'Red Velvet' Lettuce
4 plants from a multipack
Plant Profile: Page 156

Rosemary
1 plant from 6" pot
Plant Profile: Page 138

'Simpson Elite' Lettuce
4 plants from a multipack
Plant Profile: Page 156

Read this chapter carefully to avoid the many mistakes I made designing containers that include vegetables! It's really quite easy once you realize the do's and don'ts. Learn tips that teach you how to:

❀ Plant attractive vegetables alone in containers (pages 52 to 59).

❀ Plant flowers with vegetables (pages 60 to 71).

❀ Use centerpieces in the middle of mixed container combos (pages 72 to 75).

❀ Mix textures for easy success (pages 20 to 21).

❀ Use side-planted containers with vegetables (pages 76 to 89).

❀ Take care when mixing poisonous plants and vegetables (pages 90 to 91).

Left: This combo demonstrates one of the biggest lessons I learned from planting 221 containers that included vegetables: simplicity. Look how easy it is to create something attractive: Plant a rosemary in the center and surround it by lettuce in two colors!

This combo was extremely easy to care for and lasted for a full four months when I protected it from hard freezes. The lettuce wilts easily, however, when the sun shines on it. If the potting mix is wet, don't water it because it recovers on its own as the sun fades. Lettuce needs sun to grow but will take as little as four hours per day. Bowl measures 7"H x 16"D.

Some Vegetables Look Good Alone...

Vegetables that have attractive forms can look quite nice if planted in the right container. Here are some characteristics of a good looking vegetable plant:

✿ Grows fairly full to the base and not too leggy

✿ Grows fairly even

✿ Has attractive leaves

Beans (bush type), ornamental cabbages, chard, mustard greens, lettuce, okra, peppers, squash, watermelons, and tomato (bush type better) all look good alone in good-looking containers.

Above: Mustard greens look good alone in a nice container because the leaves are attractive and the form of the plant is even. I used a red pot to contrast with the lime green leaves. The pot is the 'Scallop Ring Planter' from www.pot-teryalliance.com. It measures 16 inches across. For more information on mustard greens, see page 155.

Opposite: Okra is attractive in this cobalt blue container but wouldn't look anywhere near as good in an unattractive pot. I bought this pot from a roadside vendor! It measures 16 inches across. For more information on okra, see page 158.

If Planted in Attractive Containers.

I picked 12 okra from this plant shortly after taking this photo, but I waited too long! Pick them when they are 3" to 4" long.

Squash Looks Good Alone in Great Pot.

Yellow squash (also called summer or crooked neck squash) looks fabulous all by itself in this huge, blue container. I was quite surprised at how fast it grew - from a seedling to the size shown in only six weeks! It was the first vegetable to bear fruit in my entire garden, but lasted only about two or three months. However, it produced quite a bit of squash. <u>For more detailed squash information, see page 163.</u>

I planted the same squash in mixed containers at the same time. It was much more crowded but bore fruit in about the same time period: six weeks. The fruit was smaller, and there wasn't as much of it, but it tasted good all the same.

Be sure to look under the leaves for the vegetables because they often hide!

This planting is a good example of how easy many vegetables are when planted in quite large containers. And, if you plant them in a fabulous container like this one, they are worthy of the nicest home or patio.

Male Flower

Female Flower

Cultural Information

Light: Full sun, at least six hours per day

Season: When temperatures range from 50 to 90 degrees. Optimum temperatures are 65 to 75 degrees.

Lifespan: Two to three months in this container

Care: Fertilize on planting day with a slow-release mix described on page 36. I trimmed it occasionally to keep it looking even.

Water: Water thoroughly, if the plants show signs of wilt or the soil feels dry when you push your fingertip into the potting mix (see pages 38 to 40). I watered this one every day (after it was about a month old) in mid summer and every other day in cooler weather.

Troubleshooting: Downy mildew is a problem that is hard to control (requires weekly spraying) in areas of the country that have it. It devastated this plant before I knew what had hit it. Once I understood how to control this pest, I didn't lose any more plants to it. See page 43 for more information. Squash are also sometimes bothered by squash vine borers, which bore into the stem and eat the stem from the inside out. If you see a small, black dot on the stem, cut open the stem and remove the bug.

Planting Plan: Easy. Simply plant one plant in the middle of a large pot.

Container: This container is HUGE - I don't think the photo shows how big it is. It is one of my largest, weighing in at 150 pounds! I left it outside last winter, and it didn't crack at 15 degrees. It is Campania International's *Anduze Urn* (27"W X 31"H). For best results, stick to larger containers (at least 18-inch diameter) for this type of squash for best production.

Shop for it at www.campaniainternational.com.

Best Time to Pick: When squash are small and skin is still soft. They are much more tender when small, but if you forget and leave them until the warts form, they are still edible if you cook them a little longer. See page 163 for more information.

Note: Squash flowers are edible and considered a delicacy. They bear male and female flowers (shown, left). Pick the male flowers, since they bear pollen and not fruit. Use the petals in salads.

Squash flowers bloom in the morning and are often covered by the leaves.

Look under the leaves of the plant, and you will find a lot more squash.
Plant Profile: Page 163

Watermelon Looks Good Alone.

I was amazed that watermelon grew so easily in containers! The fruit weighed about three pounds which is quite a bit smaller than the same fruit of the plant grown in the ground (eight to ten pounds). I did absolutely nothing to it after planting other than water. <u>For more detailed information about watermelon, see page 166.</u>

Icebox watermelons are smaller than traditional watermelons and were named as such because they easily fit in a refrigerator. I didn't try the large watermelons in containers, only these small ones.

The watermelons formed at the top of the plant and grew down the sides before resting on the patio. It looked like they would be too heavy for the stem and break off before hitting the ground, but that didn't happen.

One major problem arose, however. I picked the five melons too late, and they were mushy on the inside. <u>Knowing when watermelons are ready to pick can be difficult.</u> One trick is to hold your ear to the fruit and tap it with your finger. It should sound hollow, not solid.

There are nine other ways to check for watermelon ripeness. See www.almanac.com/food/watermelonripe.php or http.gardenweb.com/faq/lists/cornucop/2002071935010165.html for more tips.

Cultural Information

Light: Full sun, at least six hours per day

Season: Watermelon need warmth. Be sure to wait at least two weeks after your area's last frost date. They do best in temperatures ranging from 70 to 85 degrees, but grow in temperatures ranging from 65 to 95 degrees. More temperature information on page 166.

Lifespan: About two to three months in this container. The fruit requires two to three months of heat to mature. Once the fruit is ripe, the plant starts dying.

Care: Like most vegetables, watermelons are heavy feeders. Fertilize on planting day with a slow-release mix described on page 36. Repeat, if the leaves look yellowish or washed-out, although the fertilizer should last from six to nine months.

Water: Watermelons like quite a bit of water and are quite sensitive right after planting. I watered this one every day. See pages 38 to 40 to learn more about watering.

Troubleshooting: No problems at all. Be sure to let the watermelons fall to the ground instead of resting them on the potting mix in the container. They can rot if left on top of damp soil or potting mix.

Some watermelon plants develop fungal diseases, although ours didn't. If you see yellow or pale green spots on the leaves and think they are serious, take one to your local garden center, and ask them for the least toxic treatment. Watermelons, at times, also attract aphids.

Planting Plan: Easy. Simply plant 5 watermelon plants around the edge of a large pot. Be sure to plant in good-quality potting <u>mix</u>, not garden soil, top soil, or potting soil, which can kill your plants. Other important planting tips are shown on pages 32 to 35.

Container: This container measures 19 inches high with an inner diameter of 12 inches. The fruit probably would have grown larger in a bigger pot. Don't try it in any smaller sizes than this one.

Best Time to Pick: See the last two paragraphs at left, plus page 166.

One plant from a 4" pot
Plant Profile: Page 166

Even Tomatoes Look Good...

This design demonstrates the easiest and most attractive way to grow tomatoes. The plant is a dwarf bush tomato (Husky Cherry Red) rather than a vine tomato, and bush tomatoes are easier to control. Planting bush tomatoes with a support, like this obelisk, means you won't have to do much fooling with them to get them to stay upright as they grow taller. Use an attractive obelisk, like this one, instead of an ugly tomato cage, if you want it to look good. Also, plant in a great looking pot for a container garden worthy of the nicest patio. This arrangement wins a red ribbon because of its ease of care. I did nothing but water it after it was planted. <u>For more detailed information about tomatoes, see page 164.</u>

Making tomatoes attractive was my biggest challenge in this book, and simplicity works best.

Tomatoes grown alone in large pots (more than 16-inch diameter) get a little larger than those grown in the same size pot but are surrounded with flowers.

I was extremely happy with 'Husky Cherry Red' tomato because it bore a lot of great-tasting tomatoes and exhibited a neat growth habit. These small tomatoes are called cherry tomatoes because their size resembles cherries.

Home-grown cherry tomatoes taste much better than those you find in the grocery store.

Cultural Information

Light: Full sun, at least six hours per day. Don't even attempt tomatoes in less light.

Season: Spring through fall for most warmer areas. Best night temperatures range from 59 to 68 degrees for setting. Daytime temperatures above 90 degrees and night temperatures about 70 degrees result in less flowers and tomatoes. I was pleasantly surprised to see this one produce fruit from July until September in my Georgia garden after it was planted in June.

Lifespan: The plant actually lives for about three to four months, but the leaves start looking a bit rough after it produces quite a bit of fruit, about two months after planting from a 4-inch pot. It bears fruit for quite a while, about two months.

Care: Fertilize on planting day with a slow-release mix described on page 36. Repeat, if the leaves look yellowish or washed-out, although the fertilizer should last from six to nine months.

Water: I watered this one every day (after it was about a month old) in mid summer and every other day in cooler weather. See pages 38 to 40 to learn more about watering.

Troubleshooting: No problems at all. The leaves looked a little rough after the plant had borne lots of fruit. I left it alone.

Planting Plan: Easy. Simply plant a tomato in the middle of a large pot in good quality potting mix, not potting soil. Place the obelisk over the plant at planting time. It's harder to get it over taller plants.

Container: Masart's BTXLPR/EY-1106 (20H" x17"D). Shop for it at www.masart.com.

Best Time to Pick: Pick frequently to encourage more flowers and fruit formation. They taste best when they are allowed to ripen to a bright red color on the vine.

With Attractive Hardware and Pots.

2ND

'Husky Cherry Red' Tomato
One plant from a 5" pot
Plant Profile: Page 164

Cover Up Leggy Veggies with Flowers.

Some vegetables get leggy at the base, leaving unattractive stems that are easily seen. These include broccoli, Brussels sprouts, collards, and eggplants.

It's fast and easy to tuck some flowers in at the base, like I did with these young broccoli plants. I used violas, which are edible flowers. Look at the difference a few flowers make!

Blooper!

Before

Above: Young broccoli planted alone developed leggy stems that would be more attractive if covered by flowers. Opposite: Violas (edible flowers) are tucked in at the base. Container (11"H x 12"D x 18"W) from www.campaniainternational.com.

After

Add Flowers to Vegetables To...

Some vegetables don't look very good by themselves and need flowers added to make the entire arrangement attractive. These include arugula, beans (large, vining types), cucumbers, peas, spinach, and huge, viney tomatoes.

This spinach is a good example. It looks rather non-descript alone in the container below, but looks beautiful when combined with chrysanthemums and violas (in a larger pot) - both edible flowers. The smaller pot on this page measures 8"H x 10"W, while the larger one (shown right) is 10"H x 16"W.

Blooper!

Before

Improve Their Appearance.

After

Add Flowers to Vegetables To...

Many flowers last longer than vegetables, extending the life of the combo. This combo lived for three additional months because the flowers lived that much longer than the tomatoes.

These tomato plants produced about 32 'Better Boy' tomatoes.

Ideally, container gardens last for an entire growing season. Most vegetables, however, don't. Tomato plants, for example, only last a few months. In areas with a longer growing season, that may cut the time span for container gardens to less than half of the growing season.

Many flowering plants last much longer, with blue ribbon plants lasting as long as most growing seasons. Check out the blue ribbon flowers on pages 68 to 69.

<u>In many of my containers, with flowers that lived much longer than the vegetables, I simply cut the dead vegetable branches off and left the flowers to fill in the remaining space.</u>

I was quite delighted, over and over again, with the results, as shown with these two photographs of the same container. The one on the left was photographed in June, showing the beginnings of a nice tomato crop coming out of the bottom of this side-planted container. Lantana*, angelonia, dragon wing begonias, and sweet potato vines are planted above the tomatoes. The tomato plants produced about 32 nice fruit before dying. I simply cut off the dead branches, and left it alone. See the same container in September to the right. I moved it to another location and changed the post, but other than that, it is just the same minus the tomatoes. It looked lovely until November with just the flowers.

*Lantana are poisonous. For more information, see pages 90 and 91.

Extend the Life of the Combo.

For three-minute planting and column installation instructions, see the videos at www.sideplanting.com. Buying information on page 6.

CREATING ATTRACTIVE COMBOS 65

Add Flowers to Vegetables To...

I planted flowers around this tomato because I wanted the tomato to look good. The flowers added the additional benefit of increasing the lifespan of the container by a full three months because they lasted much longer than the tomato (although it lived long enough to produce 22 tomatoes). It qualified for a red ribbon because all I did was add water after it was planted correctly - and cut the tomato plant away when it died.

It was quite difficult to get used to mixing vegetables and flowers. I kept thinking that they looked so different and they needed to be separated. However, I realized that my attitudes were based on what I had seen, and historically, vegetables have seldom been used as part of a container design that is mainly flowers. But, as time went on and I gained experience by planting hundreds of vegetable/flower combos, I began to like the combinations that had seemed so foreign. This tomato/flower combo is one of my favorites!

Tomatoes were one of the hardest vegetables to get looking good. I planted lots that just looked awful! But, they work extremely well as a centerpiece in side-planted containers or planted in the bottom row of side holes.

The tomatoes that were planted in the top of this basket died while the other plants were still going strong. I trimmed off the dead tomato branches and the other plants filled in the resulting space, living an additional three months.

Cultural Information

Light: Full sun, at least six hours per day

Season: Warm season, when temperatures range from mid 70's to 90 degrees (tomatoes pause when the temperatures get too hot and stop producing fruit; they start again as the temperatures cool in the fall. The plants stay alive well into the mid-90's). The scaevola needs heat to grow and bloom well. Don't be surprised if it looks bad right after planting and for up to a few weeks. Afterwards, it perks up soon enough, but doesn't really take off until the weather is pretty hot. The tomato needs nights in the 70's to produce flowers.

Lifespan: The tomatoes lasted two to three months. I trimmed off their branches after they started looking bad, and the rest of the flowers lasted a total of six months (photo, below left).

Care: Fertilize on planting day with a slow-release mix described on page 36. Repeat, if the leaves look yellowish or washed-out, although the fertilizer should last from six to nine months. I trimmed it occasionally to keep it looking even.

Water: Water thoroughly, if the plants show signs of wilt or the soil feels dry when you push your fingertip into the potting mix (see pages 38 to 40). I watered this one every day (after it was about a month old) in mid summer and every other day in cooler weather.

Troubleshooting: Lantana are poisonous, so be sure not to eat them! Tomatoes have some pest problems described on page 164. The flowers are really easy, with relatively no problems.

Planting Plan: Alternate the begonias, lantana, and scaevola in the side holes and along the edge of this side-planted container. Plant the tomato as the centerpiece.

Container: Kinsman's double basket (20"W x 11"D) on a 48-inch border column. See page 6 for buying information.

Installing the Column: The 48-inch column is sold in a kit that installs easily and fits this planter well. The product number is ZGBC48. Shop for it at Kinsman Company (www.kinsmangarden.com). To see a 3.5 minute video of its installation, go to www.sideplanting.com and watch Part 6, *Patio Stands and Border Columns.*

For three-minute planting and column installation videos, see www.sideplanting.com. Buying information on page 6.

Fill Your Need for Flowers!

2ND

'Better Bush' Tomatoes
1 plant from a 5" pot
Plant Profile: Page 164

Lantana
10 plants from 4" pots
Plant Profile: Page 136

Red Dragon Wing Begonias
10 plants from 4" pots
Plant Profile: Page 130

Scaevola
10 plants from 4" pots
Plant Profile: Page 139

Easy Flowers That Look Good...

1ST

Just add water! That's all it takes to grow these vegetable companions if you follow the growing requirements shown below. Flowers (including annuals, herbs, tropicals, and perennials) that share the same growing conditions as your vegetables will thrive with them. Blue ribbon plants are the easiest. These flowers and more are covered in detail in the last chapter of this book.

More blue ribbon flowers are covered in this book's companion volume, "Easy Container Gardens."

Characteristics of Blue Ribbon Plants

✿ Dependable. Performs the same way every year.

✿ Requires little to no trimming.

✿ Adjusts to most climates.

✿ Lives a long life - at least the four to six months of your growing season.

✿ Fares well with little pest susceptibility.

✿ Established record - it's been around for enough years to fully understand it.

✿ Blooms continuously for a minimum of five to six months (except for plants used primarily for leaf color)

Growing Requirements for Blue Ribbon Plants

Dragon wing begonias and coleus, two blue ribbon plants.

✿ Use potting mix (not potting soil, top soil, or garden soil) with a brand name you trust.

✿ Use the fertilizer decribed on page 36.

✿ Be sure the pot has holes in the bottom, and don't bury the plant too deep (pages 13 and 29).

✿ Plant in the right amount of light and in the correct season, which varies per plant. Check the individual plant profiles in the last chapter of this book for specifics.

✿ Water correctly (pages 38 to 40).

With Vegetables.

Blue Ribbon Annuals, Perennials, and Herbs

Angelonia
Plant Profile: Page 130

Begonia, Dragon Wing
Plant Profile: Page 130

Begonia, Wax
Plant Profile, Page 130

Black-Eyed Susan 'Tiger Eye'
Plant Profile, Page 131

Coleus
Plant Profile: Page 132

Creeping Jenny
Plant Profile: Page 132

Crotons
Plant Profile: Page 132

Daisy, California Bush
Plant Profile: Page 133

Grass, 'Fireworks'
Plant Profile: Page 134

Grass, Fountain
Plant Profile: Page 134

Grass, Juncus
Plant Profile: Page 135

Impatiens 'Sunpatiens'
Plant Profile: Page 135

Lantana
Plant Profile: Page 136

Lavender
Plant Profile: Page 136

Melampodium
Plant Profile: Page 136

Pansies and Violas
Plant Profiles: Pages 137, 141

Purple Queen
Plant Profile: Page 138

Rosemary
Plant Profile: Page 138

Sage, Golden Variegated
Plant Profile: Page 138

Salvia, Annual
Plant Profile: Page 139

Salvia, 'Mystic Spires'
Plant Profile: Page 139

Scaevola, Blue
Plant Profile: Page 139

Sedum
Plant Profile: Page 140

Ti Plant
Plant Profile: Page 140

Know Your Priorities...

Your personal choice determines whether you use more flowers or vegetables in a container. Flower lovers often use vegetables as an accent in a container filled to the brim with flowers. People whose goal is primarily food production will mainly use vegetables.

All Vegetables

This huge (28 inches across) bowl from Tom Oswald of JAM'n Designs (www.jamndesigns.com) and Pottery Land (www.potterylandusa.com) is planted with mustard greens (plant profile, page 155) as a centerpiece, surrounded by 'Simpson Elite' and 'Mascara' lettuce (lettuce profile, page 156).

Vegetables or Flowers.

Vegetables Tucked In with Flowers

Writing this book has changed the way I will do container gardens forever. Even if I am planting a container for solely decorative impact, I will tuck in a vegetable as well. Vegetables just look great when surrounded by flowers! This container features 'Tiger Eye' black-eyed Susans surrounded by blue scaevola, red chili peppers, and creeping Jenny.

Use Centerpieces in Mixed Combos.

Plant the tallest plant in the middle and smaller plants around it. What could be easier! The big plant is called the centerpiece.

Above: Young Brussels sprouts form the centerpiece, with purple pansies and yellow violas planted in front. Pot measures 20"W x 13"H.

Opposite: Lavender forms the centerpiece, with purple ornamental kale and violas in front. Pot (16"W x 11"D x 9"H) is the 'Oval Fleur de Lis' from www.globalpottery.com.

Characteristics of Good Centerpieces

❀ A centerpiece can be any type of plant as long as it remains taller than the surrounding plants for the life of the arrangement. See pages 16 to 17 for photos of blue ribbon centerpieces.

❀ Choose a plant that is full, or combine several tall, skinny plants together so the centerpiece doesn't look too skinny.

❀ Be sure the centerpiece likes the same growing conditions (light, temperature, water) as the smaller plants going around it.

Good Centerpieces

Angelonia
Plant Profile: Page 130

Black-Eyed Susan 'Tiger Eye'
Plant Profile: Page 131

Chrysanthemum
Plant Profile: Page 131

Daisy, California Bush
Plant Profile: Page 133

Geranium
Plant Profile: Page 134

Grasses
Plant Profile: Page 134

Impatiens, 'Sunpatiens'
Plant Profile: Page 135

Lavender
Plant Profile: Page 136

Pentas
Plant Profile: Page 137

Rosemary
Plant Profile: Page 138

Salvia 'Mystic Spires'
Plant Profile: Page 139

Ti Plant
Plant Profile: Page 140

Vegetables

Broccoli
Plant Profile: Page 146

Brussels Sprout
Plant Profile: Page 147

Cabbage & Kale
Plant Profile: Page 148

Collard
Plant Profile: Page 151

Eggplant
Plant Profile: Page 154

Greens
Plant Profile: Page 155

Okra
Plant Profile: Page 158

Pepper
Plant Profile: Page 160

Tomato
Plant Profile: Page 164

Mix Textures for Easy Success.

Mixing Different Plants with the Same Sized Leaves Doesn't Work.

Blooper!

This blooper combines Swiss chard as a centerpiece surrounded by 'Redbor' kale. Although it isn't the worst combo I did, it really has no punch. The leaves look so similar that the eye doesn't differentiate between them.

Compare the visual impact of this combo to the one on the opposite page, which combines plants with leaves of very different sizes.

When you are buying plants in your garden center, be sure to shop for plants with leaves of very different sizes. A small size difference just doesn't show up. The basket is a 16-inch, single side-planted basket.

**For three-minute planting video, go to www.sideplanting.com.
Buying information for side-planted products on page 6.**

Mixing Skinny Leaves with Fat Leaves Works Well.

Skinny and fat leaves in the same arrangement work really well because the eye easily discerns the difference between the two. The skinny leaves of the Juncus grass contrasts well with the fat leaves of the ornamental cabbages. Both the pansy leaves and flowers are mid-sized. Planted in a 24-inch, side-planted, window box.

The Secret to the Instant Full Look: Flexible Side Holes*

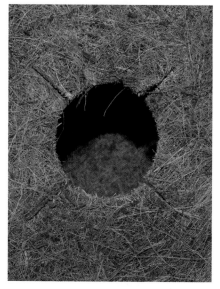

Empty basket: The holes in the sides of the baskets allow mature plants to be pushed through the sides for an instant look. This is a 16-inch basic basket on a decorative patio stand.

The hole has slits on the side, so the plant won't fall out after planting.

Soak the roots of a plant in a bucket of water. Squeeze it four to six times, and slip it through the hole. Be sure the roots are on the inside and plant is on the outside.

As Easy as 1-2-3!

Step 1: Add soil up to the first hole. Wet the root balls of the plants, and squeeze them. Slide the root balls through the holes, as shown above, right.

Step 2: Plant the centerpiece.

Step 3: Tuck in the edge plants. The finished product looks like it has been planted for months!

* Patent pending

Opposite: I moved the same basket to a border column in my garden the day I planted it. This picture was taken on planting day!

Mustard Greens
2 plants from 1-gallon pots
Plant Profile: Page 155

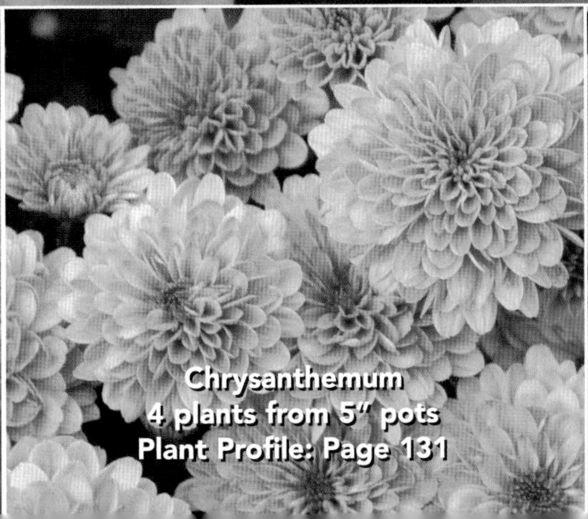

Chrysanthemum
4 plants from 5" pots
Plant Profile: Page 131

'Dynasty' Ornamental Cabbage
12 plants from 5" pots
Plant Profile: Page 148

Side Planting: Baskets, Wall Pots...

Four Types of Baskets*

 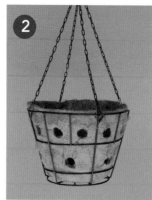

Basic baskets come with hangers, so that can be used as a hanging basket. Or, don't use the hanger, and place them on patio stands, border columns, or basket columns for large pots. Basic baskets come with either a single or double layer of holes in the sides. Single layer baskets (1) come in 14- or 16-inch diameters. Double layer baskets (2) come in 16- or 20-inch diameters.

Imperial planters are used only as hanging baskets. They also come with either single or double layers of side holes. Both are 16 inches in diameter.

Decorative cabbage as the centerpiece surrounded by chrysanthemums. Planted in a 14-inch single basic basket. Photographed the day it was planted!

* Patent pending

For three-minute planting video, go to www.sideplanting.com.
Buying information for side-planted products on page 6.

And Window Boxes Work Well.

Window Boxes and Wall Pots*

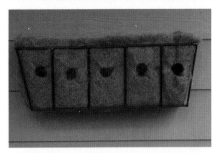

Side-planted window boxes and wall pots are extremely useful. The window boxes work well on fences or deck railings as well as under windows. Wall pots work on any wall. For easy hanging instructions, see the three-minute video at www.sideplanting.com.

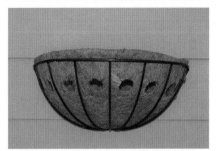

Window boxes work on walls as well as under windows. Under window: 36-inch, side-planted, window box with mustard greens and juncus grass as the centerpiece surrounded by pansies; 'Mascara' lettuce is planted in side holes. Top right: 24-inch, side-planted, window box with Juncus grass and cabbage surrounded by pansies on top; 'Dynasty' cabbage is planted in the sides. Bottom right: 30-inch, side-planted, window box with decorative kale and violas on top; mixed lettuce is planted in the sides.

* Patent pending

Side-Planting: Supports for Baskets

Basket Columns for Large Pots

Basket column kits include the hardware to convert your large pots into multi-level displays. The kits include a base ring that fits under the pot and a column that fits securely onto the ring through the drainage hole.

These were the most popular and spectacular container designs from my vegetable/flower combo trial gardens. People literally gasped when they saw them!

This grouping includes many vegetables which are hidden - see pages 26 and 27 for their locations. Large, ceramic pots from Tom Oswald of JAM'n Designs (www.jamndesigns.com) and Pottery Land (www.pottery-landusa.com).

Buying information for side-planted products on page 6.

Patio Stands

The basic baskets can be hung or supported on patio stands or columns. Patio stands come in two styles, as shown here.

For easy installation instructions, see the three minute video at www.sideplanting.com.

Left: All-In-One Combo with 16-inch, single-layer basket planted with lavender as the centerpiece, lettuce in the side holes, and violas along the edge.

Right: Ornate, ironwork, patio stand topped with 16-inch, single-layer basket planted with collard greens as the centerpiece, 'Supertunia Vista Bubblegum' petunias in the side holes, and purple violas along the edge.

Border Columns

These border columns are another alternative for supporting basic baskets. They come in kits that include a spike (that is driven into the ground), a wooden column (that fits into the spike), and a disc (to hold the basket on the column). The columns come in five heights: 24-, 30-, 36-, 42-, and 48-inches tall.

Many garden designers use these columns in sets of three, as shown opposite. These columns measure 36-, 42-, and 48-inches tall.

For easy installation instructions, see the three minute video at www.sideplanting.com.

See page 5 for more information on these plantings.

Very Important Information! Here Are...

I really blew it on most of my first attempts at using vegetables in side-planted containers. Hundreds of plants were wasted because I didn't know what to plant where. Luckily, I learned how to do it. <u>Follow these easy recommendations to the letter!</u> They show you what kind of vegetable works best in each part of these containers. If you have any questions, email me at colorgdn@aol.com. I hope my mistakes lead to your easy successes!

Three Places to Plant: Center, Edge, and Side Holes

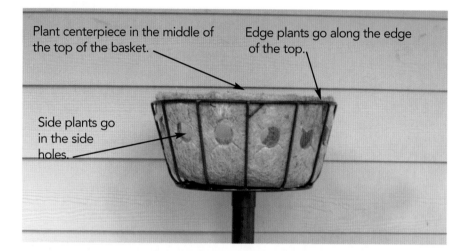

Plant centerpiece in the middle of the top of the basket.

Edge plants go along the edge of the top.

Side plants go in the side holes.

Now, this is really easy! Plant the side plants in the side holes, the centerpiece in the center of the top, and the edge plants along the edge. <u>Be sure you use the plants as I recommend here, or you could be planting your own blooper!</u>

Side Plants (For the Holes)

Cabbages or Kale, Ornamental
Plant Profile: Page 148

Cucumbers*
Plant Profile: Page 152

Eggplants, 'Ichiban'*
Plant Profile: Page 154

Lettuce
Plant Profile: Page 156

Squash and Zucchini*
Plant Profile: Page 163

Tomatoes*
Plant Profile: Page 164

*Plant long, trailing plants, like ornamental sweet potato vines, sedum, and creeping Jenny, along the edge above these plants. See pages 82 to 83 for an explanation.

The Best Vegetables for Side-Planted Containers.

Centerpieces

Arugula
Plant Profile: Page 142

Broccoli
Plant Profile: Page 146

Brussels Sprouts
Plant Profile: Page 147

Cabbages and Kale, Edible
Plant Profile: Page 148

Collards
Plant Profile: Page 151

Eggplants
Plant Profile: Page 154

Greens
Plant Profile: Page 155

Peppers
Plant Profile: Page 160

Tomatoes
Plant Profile: Page 164

Edge Plants

Cabbages or Kale, Ornamental
Plant Profile: Page 148

Lettuce
Plant Profile: Page 156

Spinach
Plant Profile: Page 156

Side-Planting Blooper...

Bare Spots on the Baskets

Blooper!

Bare spot

Before

Since I had no experience with vegetables in side-planted containers when I started this book (or anywhere else, for that matter!), I had no idea what would happen. I expected most of them to grow up from the side holes, but some of the warm-season vegetables (tomatoes, cucumbers, 'Ichiban' eggplants, melons, and squash) grew straight down.

I kept thinking the stems would break from the weight of the vegetables, but none did. However, the downward growth habit created a gap between the top of the pot and the plants, leaving the sides exposed. The point of side-planted baskets is to hide the baskets with plants, not leave them exposed. I quickly learned to plant trailing plants (like sweet potato vine - plants that REALLY grow down quite a bit) along the edge to cover up the bare pot.

The cantaloupe planted in the side holes grew straight down, exposing the side of this basket. I did a quick repair by adding some trailing plants to hide the bare spot. After this experience, I always planted trailing plants around the edge of baskets with tomatoes, cucumbers, eggplants, squash, or melons planted in the side holes. (I was not crazy about melons in the side holes. See my recommendations on pages 84 and 85.)

After soaking the root ball of the new, trailing plant (for about 5 to 10 seconds) in water, flatten it like a sandwich between your hands.

Place the root ball of the trailing plant on top of the potting mix in the side-planted container, arranging it so the plant hides the bare spot.

**For three-minute planting video, go to www.sideplanting.com.
Buying information for side-planted products on page 6.**

After

I added a few, dark purple, ornamental sweet potato plants, as well as some trailing sedum. I had no idea whether the trailing plants would live or die since I just placed the root balls on top of the potting mix and didn't really plant them. Luckily, they did quite well for months!

More Side-Planting Bloopers...

Mixing Too Many Different Vegetables in One Basket Looks Bad.

Blooper!

If you think this basket looks a little weird now, you should have seen it a month later! I made the mistake of planting both squash and tomatoes in the side holes and along the edge of this basket, alternating them with ornamental sweet potatoes and coleus. Although I did get some vegetables, the basket looked just awful, with tomato branches growing out awkwardly about two feet, and the squash looking gawky. Luckily, I learned from this experience and developed a much better method of organizing vegetables in side-planted baskets, as shown opposite.

**For three-minute planting video, go to www.sideplanting.com.
Buying information for side-planted products on page 6.**

With Solutions That Worked!

Zucchini is the only plant in the side holes of this 16-inch basket. Angelonia is the centerpiece with variegated lantana (poisonous) and wax begonias planted along the edge. The zucchini flowers were short-lived, but the vegetables followed quickly.

✿ Keep it simple! Plant just one kind of vegetable around the side holes. In a basket that has two layers of side holes, plant the vegetables in the bottom layer of holes.

✿ Plant long, trailing plants above tomatoes, cucumbers, squash, and melons.

✿ Plant a centerpiece that is taller than the rest of the plants. Vegetables work quite well as centerpieces, as well as flowers.

What About Poisonous Plants?

Take Care with Planting Poisonous Plants with Edibles

Many plants are poisonous, such as the crotons and lantana shown on these two pages. The poison will not spread from the poisonous plant to the vegetables, but you do run into the risk of someone picking a flower and eating it instead of a vegetable. That situation is most likely to happen with children.

Some plants are poisonous to eat, like lantana. Others have sap that irritates skin, such as crotons. To avoid either, look for plants listed in the last chapter of this book that have no cautions.

Below: Crotons form the centerpiece of this $5 plastic container (10"H x 16"D x 20"W). Dwarf peppers are planted in front of the center of the croton. Red ornamental peppers are planted on either side. Lantana forms the front border.

Opposite: Heliotrope (also poisonous) forms the centerpiece of this colorful Mexican pot. Dwarf peppers are planted directly in front of the heliotrope, with orange 'Sunpatiens' (new impatiens for sun) in front. Yellow lantana forms the front border. Shop for the pot at www.masart.com. 13"H x 13"D.

Chapter 3

Vegetables & Flowers: Traditional Containers

This chapter will give you ideas to re-think your container garden plans. Containers don't have to be all vegetables or all flowers. Mix them up as much as you like!

The mix depends on your priorities:

✿ Use mainly vegetables, if food is your priority.

✿ Plant mainly flowers (or plants with leaf color), if decoration is your priority.

✿ Start simply! One vegetable surrounded by one flower can create a stunning combination.

The container can make or break the overall look of the arrangement. This chapter covers some of the most glamourous ones on the market today!

Above and left: One of our vegetable gardens. Since we found that warm-season vegetables did better in large containers, these huge, frost-proof, glazed pots were ideal. Not only did the vegetables thrive (except for the corn, which died before producing much fruit), they looked great as well.

Since the pots are frost-proof, we never have to move them. We leave the potting mix in place for the winter and replace the top foot or so before planting the next spring. The center pot is so tall that we filled the bottom half with mulch instead of the more expensive potting mix.

Containers from Tom Oswald (Atlanta) of JAM'n Designs (www.jamndesigns.com) and Pottery Land (www.potterylandusa.com).

Cucumber Looks Great in a Gorgeous Pot.

This cucumber started out growing down the sides of this brown pot. I thought it might make a nice, little, trailing plant, but it grew like Jack-in-the-Beanstalk! So, I came up with the trellis idea after it was planted and mangled it considerably when attaching it to the trellis. Always put trellises or obelisks into the containers on the same day you plant! For more detailed information about cucumbers, see page 152.

Even with the manhandling the vine received, it still produced a ton of cucumbers, although many were hard to see because they hide under the leaves! The ornamental plants in front of the cucumber really worked well, since the cucumber grew as a viney backdrop for them.

Cucumbers come in vine and bush forms. Usually, the bush form is used for containers, but I couldn't find them, so I planted the vine instead. I was quite happy with its performance and plan to grow it again next spring. The only problem was downy mildew. See page 43 for remedies. Be aware that all parts of the country don't have problems with downy mildew.

Cucumbers also come as either picklers or slicers. This one is a slicer.

Large trellises like the one pictured, are really good fits for square pots. Remember to measure the pot before shopping for the trellis.

Cultural Information

Light: Full sun, at least six hours per day

Season: Cucumbers like warm weather, with a minimum temperature of 60 degrees and a maximum of 90 degrees.

Lifespan: Cucumbers last about two to four months. The ornamental plants kept going for about another four months.

Care: Fertilize on planting day with a slow-release mix described on page 36. Repeat if the leaves look yellowish or washed-out, although the fertilizer should last from six to nine months. Keep training the cucumber vine up the trellis and attach it loosely.

Water: Water thoroughly if the plants show signs of wilt or the soil feels dry when you push your fingertip into the potting mix (see pages 38 to 40). I watered this one every day.

Troubleshooting: Cucumbers grown vertically (up trellises or other supports) have better air circulation and attract fewer pests. Also, cucumbers grown in containers are less susceptible to diseases than those grown in the ground. Downy mildew is a problem that is hard to control in areas of the country that have it (requires weekly spraying). It devastated this plant before we knew what had hit it. Once we understood how to control this pest, we didn't lose any more plants to it. See page 43 for more info. Downy mildew is not present in all areas of the country and is worse in hot, wet years. See page 152 for more potential pests.

Planting Plan: Place the trellis inside the pot. Plant the cucumber in front of the trellis, and tie the branches loosely to it. Plant the grass in the center of the pot, and surround it with the other plants.

Container: Global Pottery's *Fiberglass Lattice Box.* 20H"x 20D"x 20W". This pot is not only lightweight, it also looks just like metal but doesn't rust. From www.globalpottery.com.

Best Time to Pick: Cucumbers taste best when they are medium-sized, no larger than six to eight inches long for slicers, and are grown in large pots like this one.

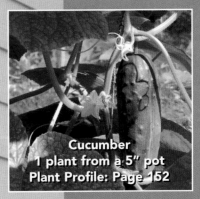

Cucumber
1 plant from a 5" pot
Plant Profile: Page 152

Cucumber Flower

'Fireworks' Grass
1 plant from a 1-gallon pot
Plant Profile: Page 134

Coleus
2 plants from 6" pots
Plant Profile: Page 132

Creeping Jenny
2 plants from a 6" pots
Plant Profile: Page 132

Great-Looking Tomato

2ND

In Chapter 2 (pages 58 to 59), I show how easy it is to grow one tomato alone in a pot and how nice it looks if you use attractive pots and hardware. This design demonstrates taking it one step further and adding a row of flowers (verbena) around the tomato to dress it up. This arrangement was incredibly easy, winning a red ribbon. For more detailed information about tomatoes, see page 164.

This tomato is called 'Husky Cherry Red.' It is one of my favorite tomatoes because it produces a lot of cherry tomatoes on a nice, neat plant.

This container is frost-proof and stays in my garden all year. It's wonderful for vegetables because of its large size. Since it stays in the garden, I plant flowers around it that coordinate with the container plants. Coleus, angelonia, purple heart, petunias, and creeping jenny are planted around the base of the container.

Making tomatoes attractive was my biggest challenge in this book, and simplicity works best. Use an attractive, large pot and attractive supports. That's all it takes!

Cultural Information

Light: Full sun, at least six hours per day. Don't even attempt tomatoes in less light.

Season: Spring through fall for most warmer areas. Best night temperatures range from 59 to 68 degrees for setting. Daytime temperatures above 90 degrees and night temperatures above 70 degrees result in less flowers and tomatoes. I was pleasantly surprised to see this one produce fruit from July until September in our Georgia garden after it was planted in June.

Lifespan: The plant actually lives for about three to four months, but the leaves start looking a bit rough after it produces quite a bit of fruit, about two months after planting from a four inch pot. It bears fruit for quite a while, about two months.

Care: Fertilize on planting day with a slow-release mix described on page 36. Repeat if the leaves look yellowish or washed-out, although the fertilizer should last from six to nine months.

Water: I watered this one every day (after it was about a month old) in mid summer and every other day in cooler weather.

Troubleshooting: No problems at all. The leaves of the tomato looked a little rough after the plant had borne lots of fruit. We left it alone. We may have just been lucky because many gardeners have more pests than that on tomatoes. See page 165 for more information.

Planting Plan: Easy. Simply plant a tomato in the middle of a large pot, and surround it with an obelisk on planting day. Plant in good quality potting mix, not potting soil. Add verbenas around the edge.

Container: 22"H x 24"W. Container from Tom Oswald (Atlanta) of JAM'n Designs (www.jamndesigns.com) and Pottery Land (www.potterylandusa.com).

Best Time to Pick: Pick frequently to encourage more flowers and fruit formation. Tomatoes taste best when they are allowed to ripen to a bright red color on the vine, although they can be picked green to keep the birds from eating them and have them ripen in your kitchen.

 Red ribbon vegetables are defined on pages 14-15.

Purple & White Verbena
2 plants from 6" pots
Plant Profile: Page 141

'Husky Cherry Red'
Tomato
1 plant from a 5" pot
Plant Profile: Page 164

Purple Verbena
2 plants from 6" pots
Plant Profile: Page 141

This arrangement was one of my favorites because it produced so many peppers and looked great all season! <u>The 'Yummy Bell' pepper had 47 peppers at once - from just one plant!</u> They stayed hidden on the back of the plant, along with the delicious 'Big Bertha' and 'Red Bell' peppers planted in this pot. From a distance, it looks like a container filled with only flowers. But, lift the leaves in back, and see the enormous numbers of peppers, as shown below. This combo deserves a blue ribbon because it took very little care. The peppers kept bearing fruit until November!

'Yummy Bell' Peppers growing under the leaves of this container combo.

**Angelonia
4 plants from 4" pots
Plant Profile: Page 130**

**Celosia
3 plants from a 4" pots
Plant Profile: Page 131**

**Creeping Jenny
6 plants from a multipack
Plant Profile: Page 132**

Cultural Information

Light: Full sun, at least six hours per day

Season: Bell peppers tolerate temperatures from 65 to 90 degrees, with optimum temperatures ranging from 70 to 80 degrees. Angelonia and celosia tolerate 45 to 95 degrees. Creeping jenny is a perennial, hardy to zone 3.

Lifespan: Five to six months in this container

Care: Fertilize on planting day with a slow-release mix described on page 36. Repeat if the leaves look yellowish or washed-out, although the fertilizer should last from six to nine months.

Keep the peppers staked so they don't fall over.

Water: Water thoroughly if the plants show signs of wilt or the soil feels dry when you push your fingertip into the potting mix (see pages 38 to 40). I watered this one every day (after it was about a month old) in mid summer and every other day in cooler weather.

Troubleshooting: No problems at all

Planting Plan: Easy. Simply plant three peppers along the back of the pot. Plant angelonia in front of the peppers and some red celosia in the center. Tuck creeping jenny along the front edge.

Container: Masart's *Belted.* (20"W x 20"H). Shop for it at www.masart.com.

Best Time to Pick: Be sure to check under the leaves because peppers hide! The more you pick, the more the plant produces. Wait until the peppers turn their mature color before removing them. Cut off the fruit and a small section of the stem with scissors.

 Blue ribbon vegetables are defined on pages 12-13.

'Yummy Bell' Pepper
1 plant from a 5" pot
Plant Profile: Page 160

'Big Bertha' Pepper
1 plant from a 5" pot
Plant Profile: Page 160

'Red Bell' Pepper
1 plant from a 5" pot
Plant Profile: Page 160

Easy and Beautiful!

2ND

This 'Husky Cherry Red' tomato was planted as an experiment to see how it would do when surrounded by really aggressive plants. I chose ornamental sweet potatoes as a companion because they are one of the most aggressive plants I know. I was pleasantly surprised to see the combination growing happily together. The tomato plant didn't get as large or produce as many tomatoes as it would have if planted alone. But, it had a respectable harvest and did surprisingly well with so much close company! For more detailed information about tomatoes, see page 164.

The combo was planted in June. The tomato lasted until late August, at which time I cut the whole plant off at the roots. The flowers and sweet potato vines continued doing beautifully until early November.

It was difficult for me to get used to mixing tomatoes with flowers because I had never seen it done before. Tomatoes are traditionally planted with other vegetables. Considering that tomato plants are not the most attractive in the world, it is nice to see how well they handle pretty, flowering companions.

I cut the tomato off at the roots when it died in August. The rest of the plants lasted another 2 1/2 months.

Cultural Information

Light: Full sun, at least six hours per day

Season: Spring through fall for most warmer areas. Best night temperatures range from 59 to 68 degrees for setting. Daytime temperatures above 90 degrees and night temperatures above 70 degrees result in less flowers and tomatoes.

Lifespan: I planted this combo in early June. The tomato plant did well until late August, at which time I cut it off at the roots. The rest of the plants lived until early November.

Care: Fertilize on planting day with a slow-release mix described on page 36. Repeat if the leaves look yellowish or washed-out, although the fertilizer should last from six to nine months.

Water: I watered this one every day (after it was about a month old) in mid summer and every other day in cooler weather.

Troubleshooting: No problems at all. The leaves of the tomato looked a little rough after the plant had borne lots of fruit. We left it alone. We may have just been lucky because many gardeners have more pests than that on tomatoes. The sweet potato vines got some holes in the leaves but not enough to warrant spraying.

Planting Plan: Plant the tomato along the back edge of the pot. Cover it with an obelisk on planting day. Surround the obelisk with layers of dragon wing begonias, heliotrope, and ornamental sweet potato vines.

Container: 22"H x 22"W

Best Time to Pick: Pick frequently to encourage more flowers and fruit formation. Tomatoes taste best when they are allowed to ripen to a bright red color on the vine, although they can be picked green to keep the birds from eating them and have them ripen in your kitchen.

Cautions: Heliotrope is poisonous.

 Red ribbon vegetables are defined on pages 14-15.

'Husky Cherry Red' Tomato
1 plant from a 5" pot
Plant Profile: Page 164

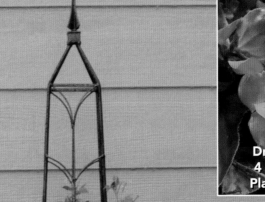

Dragon Wing Begonia
4 plants from 4" pots
Plant Profile: Page 130

Heliotrope
4 plants from 6" pots
Plant Profile: Page 135

Sweet Potato Vine
4 plants from 4" pots
Plant Profile: Page 140

Scarlet Runner Beans

It's hard to believe that the largest plant in this combo is beans! Scarlet runner beans are known as one of the longest lasting and most attractive beans. These plants also produce pretty, scarlet flowers for most of the growing season on large vines. They didn't produce as many beans in my trial gardens as pole and bush beans, but that is because my temperatures are better suited to bush and pole beans for fruiting. <u>For more information about beans, see page 142.</u>

The trellis is hard to see in this photo because it is covered by the vine. However, it is a decorative trellis, which is important for much of the season. When the vine is small and the trellis shows, the overall appearance of the combo is greatly improved with an attractive trellis.

Trellises are easier to attach to square pots than round ones.

Scarlet runner bean

Cultural Information

Light: Full sun, at least six hours per day

Season: The beans looked good the entire season (April to November) in my trial gardens but didn't produce that many beans. They prefer areas with 90 days of 60 to 85 degrees for optimum fruiting. My trial gardens are hotter than that, but the runner beans flowered throughout most of the season. The other plants lived happily for the same time period.

Lifespan: Five to six months in this container

Care: Fertilize on planting day with a slow-release mix described on page 36. Repeat if the leaves look yellowish or washed-out, although the fertilizer should last from six to nine months.

Trim the coleus to keep it looking tight. Trim the sweet potatoes and creeping Jenny to keep it even with the bottom of the pot. Keep the beans trimmed and attached to the trellis. They grow aggressively and quickly.

Water: Water thoroughly if the plants show signs of wilt or the soil feels dry when you push your fingertip into the potting mix (see pages 38 to 40). I watered this one every day (after it was about a month old) in mid summer and every other day in cooler weather.

Troubleshooting: The sweet potato vines got some holes in the leaves but not enough to warrant spraying.

Planting Plan: Place the trellis in the pot prior to planting. Plant the beans first, against the back of the pot, against the trellis. After attaching the beans to the trellis with loose ties, plant the coleus in the middle, and surround with the rest of the plants.

Be sure to plant in good-quality potting <u>mix</u>, not garden soil, top soil, or potting soil, which can kill your plants. Other important planting tips are shown on pages 32 to 33.

Container: 22"W x 22"D x 17"H

Best Time to Pick: See page 145

 Blue ribbon vegetables are defined on pages 12-13.

Scarlet Runner Bean
1 plant from a 3-gallon pot
Plant Profile: Page 144

Coleus
2 plants from 6" pots
Plant Profile: Page 132

Wax Begonia
4 plants from a multipack
Plant Profile: Page 130

'Green Yellow' Sweet Potato
2 plants from 4" pots
Plant Profile: Page 140

Creeping Jenny
2 plants from a multipack
Plant Profile: Page 132

Chapter 4

Vegetables & Flowers: $5 Containers

Most warm-season vegetables are much easier to grow in containers that are quite large. Usually, large containers are expensive. My friend Joan Ahrens and my assistant Kathy Stose went in search of budget alternatives, finding many in all kinds of different stores. The ones pictured are sold as 'party tubs' and are meant for ice and drinks. They cost $5 each. See page 29 to learn how to drill holes in the bottoms of these pots for drainage.

To support vining plants, I bought $8 wooden trellises and Kathy came up with the ingenious idea of spraying them bright colors with outdoor spray paint. After drilling some small holes in the back of the plastic pots, she used twist ties to attach the trellises to the containers, so they wouldn't fall over. Once the trellises were attached, Kathy added soil to stabilize them further.

Left: Vegetables and flowers growing in $5 containers with $8 trellises. Photo from the home of Joan and Buzz Ahrens, Canton, Georgia.

Above: Two kinds of peppers (dwarf and ornamental) tucked into a $5 container that is also planted with crotons and lantana. Both crotons and lantana are poisonous.

Dwarf Cucumber Melon

This vine was identified on the tag as a cucumber melon. I liked the vine because it was quite easy to grow - much smaller and easier to handle than either cucumbers or melons. However, the fruit production was small. That could be attributed to the fact that we didn't pick often enough!

Dwarf Cucumber Melon
2 plants from 6" pots
Plant Profile: Page 152

Zinnia
2 plants from 6" pots
Plant Profile: Page 141

Heliotrope
2 plants from 6" pots
Plant Profile: Page 135

Scaevola
2 plants from 4" pots
Plant Profile: Page 139

Cultural Information

Light: Full sun, at least six hours per day

Season: Warm season

Lifespan: The cucumber melon, heliotrope, and scaevola live for about four to five months. The large zinnias are short-lived in areas of high humidity and heat because they succumb to fungal diseases.

Care: Fertilize on planting day with a slow-release mix described on page 36. Repeat if the leaves look yellowish or washed-out, although the fertilizer should last from six to nine months. Keep the cucumber melon trimmed and trained on the trellis.

Water: I watered this one every other day in cooler weather and every day in the mid summer heat.

Troubleshooting: These large-flowered zinnias are quite susceptible to fungal diseases that create large spots on the leaves.

Planting Plan: Be sure the container has a hole in the bottom for drainage. If not, follow the instructions on page 29. In addition to a drain hole, drill a few tiny holes in the back of the plastic pot, and use twist ties to attach the trellis to the container, so it won't fall over. Once the trellis is attached, add potting mix to stabilize it further. Be sure to use good-quality potting mix, not garden soil, top soil, or potting soil, which can kill your plants. Other important planting tips are shown on pages 32 to 33.

Plant the cucumber melon along the back of the pot, and attach it to the trellis with loose ties. Add the flowers as shown in the photo.

Container: This container measures seven inches high with an inner diameter of 18 inches.

Cautions: Heliotrope is poisonous, so don't eat it!

Vining Tomato on Trellis

I planted this tomato in July with temperatures usually above 90 degrees each day. Most tomatoes stop setting fruit at these high temperatures, but the 'Heatwave' continues to bear fruit until temperatures hit the 100 degree mark. 'Heatwave' is a vining tomato that needs a support to grow well. This $8 trellis works well.

**'Heatwave' Tomatoes
1 plant from a 5" pot
Plant Profile: Page 164**

**Pentas
4 plants from 4" pots
Plant Profile: Page 137**

**Coleus
2 plants from 4" multipacks
Plant Profile: Page 132**

**Creeping Jenny
4 plants from multipacks
Plant Profile: Page 132**

Cultural Information

Light: Full sun, at least six hours per day

Season: 'Heatwave' tomatoes need heat to do well. Plant them in hot areas, where temperatures go above 90 degrees for extended periods.

Lifespan: The tomatoes lasted about three months. The ornamental plants live for an entire summer season in most of the US.

Care: Fertilize on planting day with a slow-release mix described on page 36. Repeat if the leaves look yellowish or washed-out, although the fertilizer should last from six to nine months.

Trim the coleus to keep it looking tight.

Trim the creeping Jenny if it hits the patio.

Pentas bloom more if the old flowers are removed, but I never had time to do that. Most pentas currently for sale go through periods of blooming followed by rest. They attract a lot of butterflies.

Water: Water thoroughly if the plants show signs of wilt or the soil feels dry when you push your fingertip into the potting mix (see pages 38 to 40). I watered this one every day.

Troubleshooting: No problems at all

Planting Plan: Be sure the container has a hole in the bottom for drainage. If not, follow the instructions on page 29. In addition to a drain hole, drill a few tiny holes in the back of the plastic pot, and use twist ties to attach the trellis to the container, so it won't fall over. Once the trellis is attached, add potting mix to stabilize it further. Be sure to use good-quality potting <u>mix</u>, not garden soil, top soil, or potting soil, which can kill your plants. Other important planting tips are shown on pages 32 to 33.

Plant the tomato along the back of the pot, and attach it to the trellis with loose ties. Add the flowers as shown in the photo.

Container: Called a 'party tub' in the stores. 19"L x 16"W x 9"H.

Best Time to Pick: Pick frequently to encourage more flowers and fruit formation. Tomatoes taste best when they are allowed to ripen to a bright red color on the vine, although they can be picked green to keep the birds from eating them and have them ripen in your kitchen.

Photo from the home of Joan and Buzz Ahrens, Canton, Georgia.

Collards and Edible Flowers

1ST

We found this tin container in the kitchen department of a large store. It made an attractive choice for this cool-season combo. Collards, mums, and ornamental kale are ideal fall choices for much of the country.

The flowers of the mums are edible (provided they have not been sprayed with chemicals that are not allowed on food by the FDA, which happens with some commercial growers). Use their petals on salads to add a strong taste and a little decoration. Mums bloom for a very short period, only a few weeks.

Ornamental kale, although not edible, is one of the most useful cold weather ornamentals. It lasted in my trial gardens until the temperatures dipped into the low 20's. It lives for at least six months. Most cool-season ornamentals don't last anywhere near that long. Although the leaves are edible, they don't taste very good and are more frequently used as a garnish.

Mums
2 plants from 5" pots
Plant Profile: Page 131

Collards
2 plants from 5" pots
Plant Profile: Page 151

Ornamental Kale
2 plants from 5" pots
Plant Profile: Page 164

Cultural Information

Light: Light shade (4 to 5 hours of sun per day) to full sun

Season: Collards are tolerant to moderate heat and cold, from 22 to 80 degrees. Ornamental kale prefers temperatures from 22 to 75 degrees and doesn't develop nice color until the cold arrives. Mums bloom for a very short time period in fall in most parts of the US.

Lifespan: Two to four months in this container, but the mums only bloom for about three weeks.

Care: Fertilize on planting day with a slow-release mix described on page 36. Repeat if the leaves look yellowish or washed-out, although the fertilizer should last from six to nine months.

The mums look better if you trim off the flowers after they stop blooming.

Water: Water thoroughly if the plants show signs of wilt or the soil feels dry when you push your fingertip into the potting mix (see pages 38 to 40). I watered this one every three days (after it was about a month old) and less in cold weather.

Troubleshooting: No problems at all

Planting Plan: Easy. Plant the collards along the back of the pot, centered. Plant the mums and kale as shown in the photo. Other important planting tips are shown on pages 32 to 33.

Container: Tin pot purchased in the kitchen department of a large store. 16"L x 10"W x 8"H. Be sure to drill a hole in the bottom.

Best Time to Pick: Collards can be harvested almost from the moment they have their first leaves until they are quite mature. See page 151 for more details. Pick the mum flowers or kale leaves at any time as well.

 Blue ribbon vegetables are defined on pages 12-13.

Edible Flowers, Herbs, Garnishes

1ST

The only edibles in this combo are the flowers, but the other two plants are quite useful in the kitchen. Use the kale primarily as a garnish, the rosemary for flavoring, and chomp away on the violas! This combo is extremely easy and required very little care after planting.

How do you tell the difference between ornamental kale and cabbage? Technically, both plants are in the cabbage family. However, most people call the ones with ruffled leaves ornamental kale and the ones with smooth leaves ornamental cabbage. Neither one has much color until it gets cold. Frost brings out the colors best, but they start to change at temperatures around 50 degrees. Both are actually edible but don't taste very good, so they are used much more as a garnish.

Violas are edible flowers that are commonly used in salads and as decorations for desserts.

Rosemary is commonly used as an herb in Mediterranean food as well as a flavoring with chicken and many meats.

Cultural Information

Light: Light shade (4 to 5 hours of sun) to full sun

Season: Both ornamental kale and violas are planted in fall in most areas, other than places that have very cool spring times. Ornamental kale prefers temperatures from 22 to 75 degrees and doesn't develop nice color until the cold arrives. Violas are similar. Rosemary is a perennial in zones 7 to 11.

Lifespan: Five to six months in this container

Care: Fertilize on planting day with a slow-release mix described on page 36. Repeat if the leaves look yellowish or washed-out, although the fertilizer should last from six to nine months.

Water: Water thoroughly if the plants show signs of wilt or the soil feels dry when you push your fingertip into the potting mix (see pages 38 to 40). I watered this one every three days (after it was about a month old) and less in cold weather.

Troubleshooting: No problems at all. This combo is really easy!

Planting Plan: Be sure the container has a hole in the bottom for drainage. If not, follow the instructions on page 29. The arrangement is simple! Plant the cabbage along the back, centered. Plant rosemary on either side and violas in front. Be sure to use good-quality potting <u>mix</u>, not garden soil, top soil, or potting soil, which can kill your plants. Other important planting tips are shown on pages 32 to 33.

Container: This container is sold as a 'party tub' at many stores. It measures seven inches high with an inner diameter of 18 inches.

Best Time to Pick: Anytime. Violas bloom more if frequently picked.

Blue ribbon vegetables are defined on pages 12-13.

Rosemary
2 plants from 4" pots
Plant Profile: Page 138

Ornamental Kale
1 plant from a 1-gallon pot
Plant Profile: Page 164

Violas
7 plants from a multipack
Plant Profile: Page 141

Chapter 5

Vegetables & Flowers:
Side-Planted Containers

These photos show my walkway during the trials for this book. Visitors were so surprised to realize that all of these baskets on columns included either vegetables or herbs! Side-planted containers proved to be wonderful for both. This chapter shows some of my favorites.

I made many mistakes along the way to discovering these three key guidelines:

✿ Keep it simple! Plant just one kind of vegetable around the side holes. In a basket that has two layers of side holes, plant the vegetables in the bottom layer of holes.

✿ Plant long, trailing plants above tomatoes, cucumbers, squash, and melons.

✿ Plant a centerpiece that is taller than the rest of the plants. Vegetables and flowers work quite well as centerpieces.

Take a few minutes to familiarize yourself with this revolutionary, new, planting system. See pages 76 to 89 of this book. I also made a series of short videos (no more than three minutes each) that show you how to plant and maintain these containers as well as how to install the columns you see underneath. See www.sideplanting.com for the videos. Buying information is on page 6.

Hidden Cucumbers

16" single basic basket

It is quite difficult to see all the cucumbers hiding under the leaves of this basket. Twelve were there when I took this photo, and I bet you can't see any at all! Cucumbers form quickly, so check the plant frequently after you start seeing flowers. <u>For more detailed information about cucumbers, see page 152.</u>

The only problem I had was downy mildew. See page 43 for remedies. Be aware that all parts of the country don't have problems with downy mildew.

Cucumbers come as either picklers or slicers. This one is a slicer.

The ornamental plants lasted much longer than the cucumber. I simply cut the dead vegetable branches off and left the flowers to fill in the remaining space. This practice added another four months to the life of the arrangement!

The cucumbers didn't get as large as those grown in larger containers up trellises. They grew three to four inches long and tasted great!

Container after cucumbers died. It lasted another four months!

Cultural Information

Light: Full sun, at least six hours per day

Season: Cucumbers like warm weather with a minimum temperatures of 60 degrees and maximum of 90 degrees.

Lifespan: The cucumber lasted about two months. The ornamental plants kept going for about another four months.

Care: Fertilize on planting day with a slow-release mix described on page 36. Repeat if the leaves look yellowish or washed-out, although the fertilizer should last from six to nine months.

Water: Water thoroughly if the plants show signs of wilt or the soil feels dry when you push your fingertip into the potting mix (see pages 38 to 40). I watered this one every day.

Troubleshooting: Cucumbers grown vertically have better air circulation and attract fewer pests. Also, cucumbers grown in containers are less susceptible to diseases than those grown in the ground. Downy mildew is a problem that is hard to control (requires weekly spraying) in areas of the country that have it. It devastated this plant before we knew what had hit it. Once we understood how to control this pest, we didn't lose any more plants to it. See page 43 for more info. Downy mildew is not present in all areas of the country, and is worse in hot, wet years. See page 152 for more potential pests.

Planting Plan: Plant cucumber plants in the side holes and the ti plant as a centerpiece. Alternate coleus and begonias along the top edge. See page 78 for a demonstration.

Container: Kinsman's #ZGBS16 single basket (16"W x 7"D). See page six for buying information.

Installing the Column: The 36-inch column is sold in a kit that installs easily and fits this planter well. The product number is ZGBC36. See page six for buying information. To see a three-minute video of its installation, go to www.sideplanting.com, and watch Part 6, *Patio Stands and Border Columns.*

Best Time to Pick: Cucumbers usually taste best when they are medium-sized, no larger than six to eight inches long for slicers. However, these cucumbers grew three to four inches long and tasted great!

For three-minute planting video, go to www.sideplanting.com. Buying information for side-planted products on page 6.

12 cucumbers were hiding under the leaves the day I took this photo!

Ti Plant
3 plants from 4" pots
Plant profile: Page 140

'Alabama Sunset' Coleus
4 plants from 4" pots
Plant profile: Page 132

Red Begonias
4 plants from 4" pots
Plant profile: Page 130

Cucumber
8 plants from a multipack
Plant profile: Page 152

Upside-Down Tomatoes

20" double basic basket

I planted tomatoes in 12 side-planted baskets incorrectly, which means I wasted a lot of plants. They just looked awful until I figured out a simple solution: Plant tomatoes in the bottom row of holes and plant long, trailing plants above them. This simple solution had fantastic results - a high tomato harvest and good looks!

These 'Bonnie Grape' tomatoes form a 'skirt' around the basket. It actually looks decent, and tomatoes are not attractive plants!

Growing tomatoes in the side holes of a side-planted container proved easier than in traditional containers because I didn't have to fool around with attaching it to an obelisk or trellis. I kept thinking the tomato stalks would break as they grew downward, but none did, even the ones holding larger tomatoes.

The ornamental plants lasted much longer than the tomatoes. I simply cut the dead tomato branches off and left the flowers to fill in the remaining space, as shown below. This practice added another four months to the life of the arrangement!

The tomatoes died before the rest of the plants. I simply cut the tomato branches off. The arrangement kept going another two and a half months!

Cultural Information

Light: Full sun, at least six hours per day. Don't even attempt tomatoes in less light.

Season: Spring through fall for most warmer areas. Best night temperatures range from 59 to 68 degrees for setting fruit. Daytime temperatures above 90 degrees and night temperatures above 70 degrees result in less flowers and tomatoes. I was pleasantly surprised to see this one produce fruit from July until September in our Georgia garden after it was planted in June.

Lifespan: The plant actually lives for about three to four months, but the leaves start looking a bit rough after it produces quite a bit of fruit, about two months after planting. It bears fruit for quite a while, about two months. The rest of the plants last through an entire growing season.

Care: Fertilize on planting day with a slow-release mix described on page 36. Repeat if the leaves look yellowish or washed-out, although the fertilizer should last from six to nine months. Trim the lantana and sweet potatoes to keep them neat.

Water: I watered this one every day (after it was about a month old) in mid summer and every other day in cooler weather.

Troubleshooting: No problems at all. The leaves of the tomato looked a little rough after the plant had borne lots of fruit. We left it alone. We may have just been lucky because many gardeners have more pests than that on tomatoes. See page 165 for more information. The sweet potatoes had some holes in the leaves but not enough to warrant spraying. Don't eat the lantana because it is poisonous.

Container: Kinsman's #ZGB20 double basket (20"W x 11"D). See page six for buying information.

Installing the Column: The 42-inch column is sold in a kit that installs easily and fits this basket well. The product number is ZGBC42. See page six for buying information. To see a three-minute video of its installation, go to www.sideplanting.com and watch Part 6, *Patio Stands an Border Columns.*

Best Time to Pick: Pick frequently to encourage more flowers and fruit formation. Tomatoes taste best when they are allowed to ripen to a bright red color on the vine, although can be picked green to keep the birds from eating them (and left to ripen in your kitchen).

For three-minute planting video, go to www.sideplanting.com. Buying information for side-planted products on page 6.

'Mystic Spires' Salvia
1 plant from a 6" pot
Plant Profile: Page 139

Lime Sweet Potato
6 plants from a multipack
Plant Profile: Page 140

Wax Begonias
6 plants from a multipack
Plant Profile: Page 130

Purple Sweet Potato
6 plants from a multipack
Plant Profile: Page 140

'Samantha' Lantana
6 plants from 4" pots
Plant Profile: Page 136

'Bonnie Grape' Tomato
6 plants from 5" pots
Plant Profile: Page 164

Hidden Peppers and Cucumbers

20" double basic basket

Once again, the vegetables are hiding! This combo includes both dwarf peppers and cucumbers. The cucumbers are on the top level, hanging down, while the peppers are planted in the large pot below.

The basket rests on a column kit that converts a large pot to a two-level container garden. They were the most dramatic features of our vegetable trial gardens, receiving the most 'oohs' and 'aahs' from visitors. See www.kinsmangarden.com, and look for 'Basket Columns for Large Pots' to see how they work.

Top: The cucumbers on the day I took the photo, shown right. They only grew about three to four inches long, but tasted good. They are planted in the bottom holes of the basket.

Bottom: Dwarf peppers planted in the large pot, close to the column.

Cultural Information

Light: Full sun, at least six hours per day

Season: Grow this combination of plants when temperatures range from 60 to 90 degrees.

Lifespan: Five to six months in this container. The cucumbers will only live about three months. Cut them off when they die and enjoy the rest of the plants for an additional two to three months.

Care: Fertilize on planting day with a slow-release mix described on page 36. Repeat if the leaves look yellowish or washed-out, although the fertilizer should last from six to nine months. Trim the other plants as needed to keep the arrangement neat.

Water: I watered this one every day (after it was about a month old) in mid summer and every other day in cooler weather.

Troubleshooting: Cucumbers grown vertically have better air circulation and attract fewer pests. Also, cucumbers grown in containers are less susceptible to diseases than those grown in the ground. Downy mildew is a problem that is hard to control (requires weekly spraying) in areas of the country that have it. It devastated this plant before we knew what had hit it. Once we understood how to control this pest, we didn't lose any more plants to it. See page 43 for more info. Downy mildew is not present in all areas of the country, and is worse in hot, wet years. See page 152 for more potential pests.

Planting Plan: Plant the cucumbers in the bottom row of holes. Plant the grass in the center of the top basket. Alternate coleus, begonias, and purple heart in the top row of holes and along the edge of the basket. In the bottom pot, plant the dwarf peppers in the middle, and alternate the same edge plants.

Container: Kinsman's #ZGB20 double basket (20"W x 11"D). See page six for buying information.

Basket Column for Large Pots: Kinsman's #ZPSBK. Pot must have drainage hole in the middle, or you can drill one.

Best Time to Pick: Pick the cucumbers when they seem to have stopped growing. They will be three to four inches long. Wait until the peppers turn their mature color before removing them. Cut off the fruit and a small section of the stem with scissors.

For three-minute planting video, go to www.sideplanting.com. Buying information for side-planted products on page 6.

'Fireworks' Grass
1 plant from a 6" pot
Plant Profile: Page 134

Purple Heart
9 plants from multipacks
Plant Profile: Page 138

Coleus
9 plants from multipacks
Plant Profile: Page 132

Wax Begonias
9 plants from multipacks
Plant Profile: Page 130

Coleus
9 plants from multipacks
Plant Profile: Page 132

Eggplants and Flowers

20" double basic basket

This combo was a real conversation piece. Visitors would suddenly discover the eggplants hanging down and be quite delighted to find them planted with flowers. The 'Ichiban' eggplant did quite well when planted in the bottom row of holes in this basket.

California Bush Daisy
3 plants from 6" pots
Plant profile: Page 133

Coleus
8 plants from 4" pots
Plant profile: Page 132

Lantana
8 plants from a multipack
Plant profile: Page 136

'Ichiban' Eggplant
6 plants from 5" pots
Plant profile: Page 151

Sweet Potato Vine
8 plants from a multipack
Plant profile: Page 140

Cultural Information

Light: Full sun, at least six hours per day

Season: Eggplant tolerates temperatures from 50 to 95 degrees, with optimum temperatures ranging from 70 to 85. Most eggplants need 100 to 140 days of temperatures between 70 and 90 degrees, but some are faster. See page 154 under 'Hardiness' for more information. The flowers thrive in the same temperatures.

Lifespan: Five to six months in this container. The eggplant lasted the entire time.

Care: Fertilize on planting day with a slow-release mix described on page 36. Repeat if the leaves look yellowish or washed-out, although the fertilizer should last from six to nine months. Trim the rest of the plants about once a month to keep them tidy.

Water: Water thoroughly if the plants show signs of wilt or the soil feels dry when you push your fingertip into the potting mix (see pages 38 to 40). I watered this one every day (after it was about a month old) in mid summer and every other day in cooler weather.

Troubleshooting: Both the eggplant and the sweet potato developed small holes in the leaves. We didn't spray because they weren't that noticeable. Also, lantana is poisonous, so don't eat it.

Planting Plan: Plant eggplants in the bottom row of holes. Then plant the daisies in the center. Alternate the coleus, lantana, and sweet potatoes in the top row of holes and along the edge.

Container: Kinsman's #ZGB20 double basket (20"W x 11"D). See page six for buying information.

Installing the Column: The 48-inch column is sold in a kit that installs easily and fits this basket well. The product number is ZGBC48. Buying information on page six. To see a three-minute video of its installation, go to www.sideplanting.com and watch Part 6, *Patio Stands an Border Columns.*

Best Time to Pick: Cut off the fruit with scissors to keep from damaging the plant, leaving about one inch of stem on the fruit. Timing is important because it tastes bitter if underripe or overripe. Wait until the fruit has stopped growing and has a glossy skin. Frequent harvesting stimulates more fruit production.

For three-minute planting video, go to www.sideplanting.com. Buying information for side-planted products on page 6.

12 'Ichiban' eggplants are hanging from the bottom of this basket.

16" single basic basket

Lavender and Lettuce

1ST

Lettuce is beautiful, one of the easiest vegetables to grow, and comes in many neat colors. In this combo, the lime green 'Simpson Elite' lettuce contrasts beautifully with the dark red color of the 'Red Velvet' lettuce. The lavender centerpiece forms a good textural contrast with the lettuce and violas. See page 156 for complete information about lettuce.

This combo was extremely easy to care for, requiring nothing but water after planting. It is an easy choice for a blue ribbon!

The 'Sunpatiens' planted on either side of the basket did incredibly well, blooming solidly for seven months and reaching the size of hedges!

Lavender
1 plant from a 1-gallon pot
Plant profile: Page 136

Violas
12 plants from a multipack
Plant profile: Page 141

Lettuce, 'Simpson Elite' and 'Red Velvet'
12 plants from multipacks
Plant profile: Page 156

Cultural Information

Light: Partial shade (four to five hours of sun) to full sun

Season: Cool season. Lettuce grows best in temperatures ranging from 45 to 80 degrees. See page 157 under 'Hardiness' for more information. The other plants are compatible with the same temperature range.

Lifespan: Two to four months in this container

Care: Fertilize on planting day with a slow-release mix described on page 36. Repeat if the leaves look yellowish or washed-out, although the fertilizer should last from six to nine months.

Water: Water thoroughly if the plants show signs of wilt, or the soil feels dry when you push your fingertip into the potting mix (see pages 38 to 40). I watered this every day when it was first planted and every two to three days once it was established and the weather was cooler.

Troubleshooting: Lettuce wilts easily, even when it isn't thirsty - particularly when the sun hits it. If it wilts and the potting mix is wet, don't water it again that day. It will recover on its own in a little while.

Planting Plan: Alternate the two different lettuces in the side holes. Plant the lavender in the top. Tuck the violas in around the edge. See page 78 for a demonstration, or go to www.sideplanting.com for a three-minute video demo.

Container: Kinsman's #ZGBS16 single basket (16"W x 7"D). See page six for buying information.

Installing the Column: The 36-inch column is sold in a kit that installs easily and fits this planter well. The product number is ZGBC36. See page six for buying information. To see a three-minute video of its installation, go to www.sideplanting.com and watch Part 6, *Patio Stands and Border Columns.*

Best Time to Pick: These two varieties of lettuce are leaf lettuce and are ready at any time. Cut off the outer leaves so the rest of the plant remains intact and keeps producing.

For three-minute planting video, go to www.sideplanting.com. Buying information for side-planted products on page 6.

Pretty and Entirely Edible!

30" window box

Everything in this container is edible, even the kale that looks so ornamental! The lettuce planted in the sides is sold as 'Mixed Lettuce,' which results when growers plant lots of different kinds of lettuce seeds in the same small, nursery pots. It was my favorite lettuce to plant when I wanted lots of different kinds in one pot. Even the violas are edible, commonly used in salads and as a decoration for desserts.

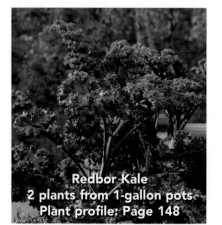

Redbor Kale
2 plants from 1-gallon pots
Plant profile: Page 148

Violas
12 plants from a multipack
Plant profile: Page 141

Mixed Lettuce
8 plants from 4" pots
Plant profile: Page 157

Cultural Information

Light: Partial shade (four to five hours of sun) to full sun

Season: Cool season. Lettuce grows best in temperatures ranging from 45 to 80 degrees. See page 157 under 'Hardiness' for more information. The other plants are compatible with the same temperature range and will take it quite a bit colder.

Lifespan: Three to four months in this container

Care: Fertilize on planting day with a slow-release mix described on page 36.

Water: Water thoroughly if the plants show signs of wilt or the soil feels dry when you push your fingertip into the potting mix (see pages 38 to 40). I watered this every day when it was first planted and and every two to three days once it was established and the weather was cooler.

Troubleshooting: Lettuce wilts easily, even when it isn't thirsty - particularly when the sun hits it. If it wilts and the potting mix is wet, don't water it again that day. It will recover on its own in a little while.

Planting Plan: Plant containers of mixed lettuce in the side holes. Plant the kale in the center, and surround it with violas.

Container: Kinsman's #CLZW30 window box (30"L x 8"W x 8"D). See page six for buying information.

Hanging the Window Box: This one is just perched on top of a deck railing, which is not recommended because it can easily fall. To learn how to attach a window box to a deck railing or under a window, see the three-minute video demonstration at www.sideplanting.com.

Best Time to Pick: Cut off the outer leaves (of both the lettuce and the kale) so that the rest of the plants remain intact and keep producing. Lettuce leaves can be picked at anytime. Kale leaves can be picked from the time they are three inches long.

For three-minute planting video, go to www.sideplanting.com. Buying information for side-planted products on page 6.

Chapter 6

Vegetables & Flowers: Growing Information

This chapter includes results of many years of plant trials with flowers and ornamental plants. It takes the guesswork out of choosing many plants from your garden centers, describing both the good and the bad about them. Take it with you, so you can check them out before you buy them. If you want information on more flowers, check out the books' companion, "Easy Container Gardens."

This chapter also covers the top 18 vegetables from my extensive, one-year trials. The vegetable information is critical to your choices prior to purchasing. Take it with you to the garden center, so you will not make as many mistakes as I did! Know the following BEFORE buying a vegetable for a container:

✿ How large the vegetable grows in containers

✿ How easy the vegetable is to grow

✿ What the correct season is for the vegetable

✿ How many vegetables one plant can produce?

Although this book doesn't cover every kind of vegetable (there are 25,000 different kinds of tomatoes!), it gives you a great start on successful container growing of both vegetables and flowers.

Above: Coleus and a dragon wing begonia

Left: Habenero peppers, dragon wing begonias, and coleus

Plant Profiles: Flowers and Ornamentals

Angelonia

Angelonia has been an erratic bloomer in my trials except for the 'Serena' series, which bloomed constantly for seven months with no care other than water!

Care: Plant with slow-release fertilizer described on page 36, and leave them alone!

Water: Medium. Up to every day in hot summers.

Season: When temperatures range from 45-100 degrees.

Light: Full sun to light shade

Zone: Protect from freezes

Pest problems: None known

Use: Centerpiece or accent

Size: Varies from 8"-18" tall

Colors: White, pink, different shades of lavender.

Average life: The 'Serena' series lasts about 6 months, blooming constantly. Some of the others I tried lasted only a month or so. Many others live for 6 months but go in and out of flowers.

Cautions: None known

Begonia, Dragon Wing

Dragon wing begonias are one of the highest performers in my trials, blooming continually with an impressive percentage of color for at least 6 months.

Care: Very easy. Plant with slow-release fertilizer described on page 36. Trim off the tips if the plants become too large.

Water: Medium

Season: Any frost-free season

Light: Medium shade to full sun. Needs some break from sun if temperatures stay consistently above 94 degrees.

Zone: Use as an annual. Tolerant of light frost but not a freeze.

Pest problems: Occasional fungus, caterpillars, or snails.

Use: Mounding or centerpiece plant. One of the best plants for the sides of a side-planted container.

Size: In the top of a large container, grows 2' tall by 1' wide. Smaller if planted in the side of a basket, about 8" tall.

Colors: Red or pink

Average life: 6-12 months, if protected from frost. One season in most areas.

Begonia, Wax

Wax begonias are one of the highest performers in my trials. They never go out of bloom and live happily for a full, 6 month period.

Care: Very easy. Plant with slow-release fertilizer described on page 36, and leave them alone!

Water: Low, but tolerates daily watering if planted with impatiens.

Season: Any frost-free season. Prefers temperatures below the high-90's.

Light: Medium shade to full sun in the cooler areas, but some burn in the summer sun. Bronze-leafed varieties, as well as new, sun-tolerant, green ones, are more sun-tolerant in the heat.

Zone: Use as an annual. Tolerant of light frost but not a freeze.

Pest problems: Occasional fungus, shown by leaf spots.

Use: Mounding plant

Size: In the top of a container, grows about 8" tall by 5" wide. Smaller if planted in the side of a basket, about 4"-6" inches tall.

Colors: Red, pink, or white flowers on green or bronze leaves.

Average life: 5-6 months

 Blue ribbon flowers are defined on pages 68-69.

Black-Eyed Susan 'Tiger Eye'

This new black-eyed Susan blooms for most of the season with very little care. I was very impressed with the color impact of this annual black-eyed Susan.

Care: Very easy. Plant with slow-release fertilizer described on page 36, and leave them alone! Fertilize again in 6-9 months.

Water: Medium. I watered mine twice a week in cool weather and daily in hot weather in containers.

Season: When temperatures range from 45-100 degrees.

Light: Full sun, at least 6 hours per day.

Zone: Use as an annual.

Pest problems: None in my trials

Use: Centerpiece or accent

Size: The different types average 12"-18" tall by 6"-12" wide.

Colors: Gold flowers with a dark brown center.

Average life: One growing season.

Cautions: None known

Celosia

Celosia are one of the highest performers in my trials, blooming continually with an impressive percentage of color for at least 4-6 months.

Care: Very easy. Plant with slow-release fertilizer described on page 36, and leave them alone! Fertilize again in 6-9 months. Trim off the tips if the plants become too large.

Water: Medium

Season: Any frost-free season

Light: Light shade to full sun

Zone: Use as an annual.

Pest problems: None known

Use: Centerpiece plant. Not good for sides of side-planted containers.

Size: Size depends on type. I grew mainly the red one shown in the photo. In the top of a large container, grows 18" tall by about 8" wide. Smaller sized celosia didn't last as long for us.

Colors: Red, pink, orange, yellow. The red did best for us.

Average life: One growing season.

Chrysanthemum

Chrysanthemums bloom in the fall and are so gorgeous they are hard to resist! Edible flowers. Bloom for a very short time, only a few weeks.

Care: Very easy. Plant with slow-release fertilizer described on page 36, and leave them alone!

Water: Medium, but tolerates daily watering if planted with impatiens.

Season: Flowers in fall. Lives on as a perennial in many areas.

Light: Full sun, at least 6 hours per day.

Zone: Use as an annual. Tolerant of light frost but not a freeze.

Pest problems: Occasional fungus, shown by leaf spots.

Use: Mounding plant

Size: 6"-24" tall and equally as wide.

Colors: White, purple, red, yellow, purple.

Average life: 5- 6 months

Cautions: Some commercially grown plants have been sprayed with chemicals that are not allowed by the FDA on food.

Plant Profiles: Flowers and Ornamentals

Coleus

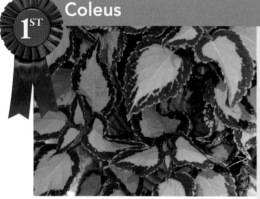

Coleus are one of the highest performers in my trials, thriving as centerpieces or planted in the sides. They come in a fascinating array of colors and patterns.

Care: Very easy. Plant with slow-release fertilizer described on page 36. Pinch the tips monthly if plant becomes too large. If you delay this trimming, it may take them a while to look good again.

Water: Medium

Season: Whenever temperatures are above 38 degrees.

Light: Light shade to full sun

Zone: Use as an annual

Pest problems: Occasional aphids, mites, mealybugs, slugs, and snails.

Use: Smaller types for mounding plants and larger ones for centerpieces. Does quite well planted through the side holes of a side-planted container.

Size: Varies greatly by variety, 6"-36" tall and equally as wide.

Colors: Shades of red, white, yellow, and green and purple.

Average life: 6 months

Cautions: Unknown

Creeping Jenny

Creeping Jenny is one of the best trailing plants for containers. It is easy to grow - and quick to reach a good size without overwhelming the other plants.

Care: Very easy. Plant with slow-release fertilizer described on page 36 and fertilize again in 6-9 months. Trim off the tips if the plants become too large.

Water: Medium

Season: All year in frost free areas. Dies back in a frost but returns in zones 3-11.

Light: Medium shade to full sun

Zone: 3-9 as a perennial. Use as an annual in zones 10-11.

Pest problems: None known

Use: Trailing plant. Does quite well planted through the side holes of a side-planted container.

Size: Trails over the edge of the pot to at least 18", but it takes a while to get there!

Colors: Lime green

Average life: Long term perennial in zones 3-9.

Cautions: Unknown

Croton

Crotons are one of the easiest plants for containers. They are happy in the same pot for years on end and require little care. There are hundreds of different varieties, all of which take heat well.

Care: Very easy. Plant with slow-release fertilizer described on page 36, and leave them alone! Fertilize again in 6-9 months.

Water: Medium

Season: Use when temperatures range from 40 to over 100 degrees.

Light: Medium shade to full sun

Zone: 10a to 11 for outside. In cooler zones, move containers inside if cold threatens.

Pest problems: Occasional scale, mealybugs, and spider mites.

Use: Centerpiece or mounding plant.

Size: Varies greatly by variety, from dwarfs to small trees.

Colors: Shades of red, yellow, green, pink, grey, black, and orange.

Average life: 15 to 20 years. Plant in your garden (in frost-free areas) when it outgrows your container.

Cautions: Milky sap irritates skin and stains clothes.

 Blue ribbon flowers are defined on pages 68-69.

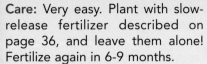

Daisy, California Bush

California bush daisy (yellow flower, above) is one of the highest performing daisies from my trials. It blooms almost continuously for at least 6 months.

Care: Very easy. Plant with slow-release fertilizer described on page 36, and leave them alone! Fertilize again in 6-9 months.

Water: Medium

Season: Prefers temperatures between 35 and 90 degrees.

Light: Light shade to full sun

Zone: Although this plant is used as a perennial in other warm parts of the world, it performs best as an annual in most areas. Protect from frost.

Pest problems: Spider mites occasionally. I have never had a pest on this plant in my gardens.

Use: Centerpiece or accent

Size: About 18" tall by 12" wide

Colors: Yellow

Average life: Looks good for about 6 months in the same container.

Cautions: Unknown

Dusty Miller

Dusty Miller is an excellent annual - easy and dependable. Doesn't do well in the sides of side-planted containers, but thrives along the edges. Likes cooler temperatures and lives all winter in warm climates.

Care: Very easy. Plant with slow-release fertilizer described on page 36 and fertilize again in 6-9 months. Trim off the tips if the plants become too large.

Water: Medium

Season: Zones 4-7 in summer; in winter, it does well in zones 8-10.

Light: Light shade to full sun

Zone: Zones 4-7 in summer; in winter, it does well in zones 8-10.

Pest problems: In very warm, rainy years, it may be troubled by root rot diseases.

Use: Upright plant. Doesn't do well planted in the side holes of side-planted baskets.

Size: 6"-12" tall, equally as wide. Size is proportional to container size.

Colors: Silver

Average life: 4-7 months. Occasionally lives up to one year in the ground.

Cautions: All parts of the plant are poisonous when eaten.

Euphorbia 'Diamond Frost'

Euphoria 'Diamond Frost' has taken the container garden market by storm! Great, light texture that contrasts well with most vegetables.

Care: Very easy. Plant with slow-release fertilizer described on page 36, and leave them alone! Fertilize again in 6-9 months.

Water: Low to medium

Season: Use when temperatures range from 40 to over 100 degrees.

Light: Full sun

Zone: Use as an annual.

Pest problems: None in my trials

Use: Centerpiece or mounding plant.

Size: The larger the container, the larger the plant. From 8"-24" tall.

Colors: White

Average life: One season

Cautions: Milky sap irritates skin and causes stomach discomfort if eaten.

Plant Profiles: Flowers and Ornamentals

Geranium

Geraniums look better with the dead flowers removed. They thrive in containers and are one of my best choices for centerpieces.

Care: Plant with the fertilizer described on page 36. Geraniums look better with the dead flowers removed, which can be tedious. I sometimes let them go and am surprised at how well they do!

Water: Medium to low

Season: Prefers temperatures between 35 and 90 degrees.

Light: Light shade to full sun

Zone: Although this plant is used as a perennial in other warm parts of the world, it performs best as an annual in most areas. Protect from frost.

Pest problems: Spider mites occasionally. I have never had a pest on this plant in my gardens.

Use: Centerpiece or accent

Size: 12"-14" tall

Colors: Many shades of red, pink, peach, white, and lavender.

Average life: 5-6 months

Cautions: Unknown

Grass, Fireworks

'Fireworks' Grass is a fabulous, new grass that is multi-colored (burgundy and hot pink) and simple to grow! Great centerpiece surrounded by vegetables.

Care: Very easy. Plant with slow-release fertilizer described on page 36, and leave it alone!

Water: Low

Season: Plant when temperatures vary between 35 degrees and the low-100's. This plant is an annual in all zones except 9-11.

Light: Light shade to full sun

Zone: Use as an annual except in zones 9-11.

Pest problems: None known

Use: Centerpiece

Size: Grows about 18" tall in a large container.

Colors: Burgundy and hot pink

Average life: 6 months, or during one growing season except in zones 9-11, where it is a perennial lasting several years.

Cautions: Unknown

Grass, Fountain

Fountain grass has a tall, graceful form. It looks good when not blooming but better when the fuzzy seed fronds form. They last a month or so. Caring for fountain grass is easy.

Care: Very easy. Plant with slow-release fertilizer described on page 36, and leave them alone! Fertilize again in 6-9 months.

Water: Low

Season: Protect from frost because it dies back in freezing weather.

Light: Light shade to full sun

Zone: Hardy to zone 4

Pest problems: None known in pots.

Use: Centerpiece

Size: In the top of a container, grows about 3' by 2.5' wide.

Colors: Green, bronze, gray

Average life: 6 months

Cautions: Unknown

Blue ribbon flowers are defined on pages 68-69.

Grass, Juncus

1ST

Juncus is one of the best grasses for centerpieces. Its tall stature keeps it well above most plants used for edge plantings. And, it is incredibly easy to grow!

Care: Very easy. Plant with slow-release fertilizer described on page 36, and leave them alone! Fertilize again in 6-9 months.

Water: Low to high. Very adaptable to what is needed by the plants around it.

Season: Dies back somewhat when the temperatures hit the low 20's. Best used in spring, summer, and fall.

Light: Light shade to full sun

Zone: Hardy to zone 4

Pest problems: None known

Use: Centerpiece or accent

Size: 15"-24" tall

Colors: Green

Average life: Perennial to zone 4. Exact lifespan unknown.

Cautions: Unknown

Heliotrope

Heliotrope surprised me last summer by really doing well in the Georgia heat! I had only seen it in cool temperatures previously. Give it a try! The color is gorgeous!

Care: Very easy. Plant with slow-release fertilizer described on page 36, and leave them alone!

Water: Medium

Season: Use as an annual. Won't take freezes.

Light: Light shade to full sun

Zone: Grow as an annual.

Pest problems: None known in pots.

Use: Centerpiece or accent. Too large for side holes of side-planted containers.

Size: In the top of a container, grows about 18" tall by 14" wide.

Colors: Purple

Average life: 3-6 months

Cautions: Poisonous. Do not eat this plant.

Impatiens 'Sunpatiens'

1ST

'Sunpatiens' are the best kind of impatiens I have ever grown. They grow in the sun and produced more color than any other plant in my trial garden last summer!

Care: Very easy. Plant with slow-release fertilizer described on page 36, and leave them alone!

Water: High, but not as high as regular impatiens.

Season: Use as an annual. Grows much faster after temperatures hit the 80's.

Light: Light shade to full sun

Zone: Use as an annual.

Pest problems: I had no pests in my trials. I didn't touch the plants at all after the initial planting and fertilization.

Use: Centerpiece, edge, or side plant. Did beautifully in the sides of side-planted containers.

Size: Grew 8"-16" tall in containers, much taller in the ground.

Colors: Peach, white, hot pink, red, purple.

Average life: 4-7 months

Cautions: Unknown

Plant Profiles: Flowers and Ornamentals

Lantana

Lantana grow well in hot, dry areas. Look for older varieties. Some of the new ones I tried went in and out of bloom. Excellent for hot temperatures and lots of butterflies.

Care: Very easy. Plant with slow-release fertilizer.

Water: Medium in containers. Low in the ground.

Season: Purple peaks in temperatures from 32-85 degrees. Other colors peak in temperatures from 70 to the low 100's.

Light: Light shade to full sun

Zone: Use as an annual. Some grow as perennials to zone 8.

Pest problems: Occasional fungus and whitefly. Do not over water.

Use: Trailing or mounding varieties.

Size: Expect trailers to grow 12" down the edge of the pot. The upright variety will grow 2' tall in a pot.

Colors: Yellow, purple, red, orange, white.

Average life: 2-4 months in container.

Cautions: Poisonous to humans and pets. Can cause serious illness or death.

Lavender

Lavender grows extremely well as a centerpiece in containers. Purple flowers are lovely, but foliage looks great even when plant is not blooming.

Care: Easy. Plant with slow-release fertilizer described on page 36, and leave them alone!

Water: Medium in containers. Low in the ground.

Season: Blooms in summer.

Light: Full sun

Zone: Perennial in zones 5-10

Pest problems: Occasional fungus.

Use: Centerpiece

Size: 20"-24" in the ground; slightly smaller in containers.

Colors: Greenish-grey foliage with purple flowers.

Average life: 6 months in container. Perennial in zones 5-10. Doesn't last too long in wet areas.

Cautions: Fungus a problem in hot, humid areas; new varieties have been developed that are less susceptible; check with local growers and www.bonnieplants.com.

Melampodium

Melampodium is one of my favorite, yellow-flowering container plants. It blooms well all summer. The daisy-like flowers add a mass of yellow to any arrangement.

Care: Very easy. Plant with slow-release fertilizer described on page 36, and leave them alone!

Water: Medium

Season: Summer. It does not like temperatures lower than 50 degrees.

Light: Medium shade to full sun

Zone: Use as an annual

Pest problems: Occasional fungus

Use: Mounding plant for sides and edges.

Size: 12"-36" tall by equally as wide.

Colors: Yellow

Average life: 5-6 months

Cautions: Unknown

 Blue ribbon flowers are defined on pages 68-69.

Pansy

Pansies are great for cool weather containers, where you can see the detail of those faces you often miss when they're planted in the garden. They are edible and extremely easy to grow.

Care: Very easy. Plant with slow-release fertilizer described on page 36, and leave them alone!

Water: Medium. Water less in cooler weather, but don't let them go into a dry, cool spell with dry potting mix.

Season: Prefer temperatures from 20-80 degrees. Don't look great at 20 degrees, but recover quickly when it warms up.

Light: Light shade to full sun

Zone: Different varieties have different cold tolerances.

Pest problems: Occasional slugs or aphids.

Use: Mounding plants for sides and edges.

Size: 4"-6" tall by about 6" wide.

Colors: White, yellow, purple, brown, blue, pink, red, multicolors.

Average life: 4-6 months in containers.

Cautions: Unknown

Pentas

Pentas bloom for most of the summer, but don't rate a ribbon because many of the ones commonly sold now periodically go out of bloom. They are great for butterflies.

Care: Plant with the fertilizer described on page 36, and leave them alone! Plants bloom more if you remove the dead flowers.

Water: Medium

Season: Any frost-free season. Takes high temperatures well.

Light: Light shade to full sun

Zone: Grown all over the world as a summer annual. Frost sensitive.

Pest problems: Mites

Use: Centerpiece or accent

Size: 12"-18" tall in containers

Colors: Red, white, purple, or pink

Average life: 3-5 months

Cautions: Unknown

Note: I had consistent good luck with the older varieties of pentas. They never went out of bloom.

Some of the newer varieties are so dense they trap moisture and die quickly from fungus.

Petunia

Petunias are one of the most popular container plants in the world. However, many of the unnamed varieties are quite short lived, so they don't rate a ribbon.

Care: Plant with slow-release fertilizer described on page 36. Remove the dead blooms if you have time.

Water: Medium

Season: Different varieties take different temperatures. None take freezing weather.

Light: Light shade to full sun

Zone: Use as an annual. Tolerant of light frost but not a freeze.

Pest problems: Fungus and whiteflies.

Use: Mounding or trailing plant that works well along the edges. Tricky in the sides of side-planted baskets.

Size: All stay quite low, about 6" tall. Trailing varieties vary in spread, up to 3'.

Colors: Red, purples, white, yellow, pink.

Average life: 1-6 months

Cautions: Unknown

Plant Profiles: Flowers and Ornamentals

Purple Heart or Purple Queen

Purple heart is one of the toughest container plants, taking heat, drought, and salt. However, it sticks out awkwardly sometimes.

Care: Very easy. Plant with slow-release fertilizer described on page 36, and leave them alone!

Water: Low, but adapts to more water if planted with more thirsty plants.

Season: Lives as a perennial in zones 7-10. Used as an annual elsewhere. Dies back in a freeze wherever it is planted.

Light: Light shade to full sun. Loses color in too much shade.

Zone: Zones 7-10

Pest problems: None known

Use: Accent. I'm not crazy about it in the side holes of side-planted containers because it sticks out awkwardly, but I use it when I can't find any other plant of this color.

Size: 10"-14" tall by 8" wide

Colors: Purple

Average life: About 6 months in a container.

Cautions: Sap is an irritant.

Rosemary

Rosemary is an herb that is a useful centerpiece because of its durability and vertical shape. Comes in upright, spreading, or prostrate forms, so be sure you know what you are buying.

Care: Very easy. Plant with slow-release fertilizer described on page 36, and leave them alone! Fertilize again in 6-9 months.

Water: Low in the ground, but adapts to high water in container gardens with good quality potting mix.

Season: Protect from frost. Takes heat very well.

Light: Full sun, at least 6 hours per day.

Zone: 7-11. Lives longer in dry areas.

Pest problems: None known

Use: Use upright forms for centerpieces, spreading forms for accent plants.

Size: 18"-48" tall in a container, usually about 24."

Colors: Green, silvery green.

Average life: Years in zones 7-11. Used as an annual for one growing season in other areas.

Cautions: None known

Sage, Golden Variegated

This useful sage is one of the few herbs with decorative leaves. It is also extremely easy to grow, thriving in every container planted!

Care: Very easy. Plant with slow-release fertilizer described on page 36, and leave them alone!

Water: Medium, but adapts to daily watering in containers.

Season: Plant when temperatures vary between 32 degrees and the low 100's.

Light: Full sun, at least 6 hours per day.

Zone: Use as an annual outside of zones 7-10. Short-lived as a perennial.

Pest problems: None known

Use: Edge plant. Also does extremely well planted in the holes of side-planted containers.

Size: Grows about 8" tall and equally wide in a container.

Colors: Bright green, lime green, variegated with both colors.

Average life: 6-7 months

Cautions: Unknown

Blue ribbon flowers are defined on pages 68-69.

Salvia, annual

Annual salvias are useful centerpiece plants for containers. They not only bloom for 5-6 months without stopping but also offer spiky flowers that contrast well with round ones.

Care: Very easy. Plant with slow-release fertilizer described on page 36, and leave them alone!

Water: Medium

Season: Any frost-free season. Requires more maintenance in hot temperatures. The dead blooms need to be removed.

Light: Light shade to full sun

Zone: Use as an annual

Pest problems: I have never seen a pest on these plants but have heard of occasional thrips, mites, caterpillars, and slugs.

Use: Centerpiece or accent

Size: In the top of a container, the blue grows 15"-18" tall. The red grows about 8"-12" tall.

Colors: Many shades of white, red, peach, and purple.

Average life: 5-6 months

Cautions: Unknown

Salvia, 'Mystic Spires'

Salvia 'Mystic Spires' is the best blue salvia I have found for containers. It grows compactly and doesn't fall over like some of the perennial blue salvias.

Care: Very easy. Plant with slow-release fertilizer described on page 36, and leave them alone! Remove dead flowers if you have the time.

Water: Medium

Season: Plant when temperatures vary between 32 degrees and the low 100's.

Light: Light shade to full sun

Zone: Use as an annual

Pest problems: None known

Use: Centerpiece or accent

Size: 12"-18" tall

Colors: Blue

Average life: 6 months

Cautions: Unknown

Scaevola

Scaevola blooms non-stop in temperatures from 45 to the low-100's. And, it lives for at least 7 months with no care other than water! Have patience in spring, however. This plant needs heat about 85 degrees to grow thickly.

Care: Very easy. Plant with slow-release fertilizer described on page 36, and leave them alone!

Water: Low

Season: Plant when temperatures vary between 45 degrees and the low 100's.

Light: Light shade to full sun

Zone: Use as an annual

Pest problems: None known

Use: Trailing plant. Does quite well planted through the side holes of a side-planted container.

Size: Trails up to 36" down the sides of a container.

Colors: White or blue

Average life: 6-7 months

Cautions: Unknown

Plant Profiles: Flowers and Ornamentals

Sedum 'Angelina'

Sedum 'Angelina' is the plant I use whenever I am stumped over what to put in a pot. When I get down to the final touches and need just one more plant, sedum always works.

Care: Very easy. Plant with slow-release fertilizer described on page 36, and leave them alone!

Water: Low, but adapts to more water if planted with more thirsty plants.

Season: Plant when temperatures vary between 32 degrees and the low 100's.

Light: Light shade to full sun

Zone: 3-11

Pest problems: I've never encountered any, but I've heard of occasional aphids.

Use: Mounding plant

Size: About 3" tall by 6"-8" wide

Colors: Lime green

Average life: 6 months as a decorative container plant because it dies back in cold temperatures.

Cautions: Unknown

Sweet Potato, Ornamental

Ornamental sweet potatoes are the fastest-growing, trailing plant in this book! Edible tubers, but not nearly as tasty as regular sweet potatoes. Gets lots of holes in the leaves, but I usually don't spray.

Care: Plant with the fertilizer described on page 36. Trim monthly, or it will completely take over the container.

Water: Medium

Season: Plant when temperatures vary between 45 degrees and the low-100's.

Light: Medium shade to full sun

Zone: Use as an annual.

Pest problems: Snails, Japanese beetles, fungus, aphids, and white flies occasionally. I have given up on trying to spray this plant and just put up with small holes in the leaves. I spray only when something is completely devouring it.

Use: Trailing plant

Size: They know no bounds...literally, they'll shoot out ten feet!

Colors: Lime green, purplish-black, and pink.

Average life: 6 months

Cautions: Unknown. Produces a sweet potato some eat but most don't like.

Ti Plant

Ti Plants are one of the most useful centerpiece plants for container gardens. Their upright, spiky form contrasts well with round leaves and flowers. And, they are simple to grow.

Care: Very easy. Plant with slow-release fertilizer described on page 36, and leave them alone! Fertilize again in 6-9 months.

Water: Medium

Season: Any frost free season (See 'Zone').

Light: Medium shade to full sun, depending on variety.

Zone: For most ti plants, use as an annual unless you live in a frost-free area. Some tis take temperatures down to the mid 20's.

Pest problems: If holes appear in the leaves, it is probably snails. I don't put out any snail bait unless the damage is extensive.

Use: Centerpiece or accent

Size: Varies by type. Most grow to about 2' tall in a typical container.

Colors: Shades of red, pink, and green.

Average life: 6 months

Cautions: Unknown

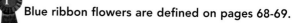

Blue ribbon flowers are defined on pages 68-69.

Verbena

Verbena are primarily used as annuals, although a few perennial types exist. They come in trailing and upright forms. I've done better with the trailers, but they go in and out of bloom.

Care: Plant with slow-release fertilizer described on page 36.

Water: Medium

Season: Plant when temperatures vary between 32 degrees and the low 80's.

Light: Full sun

Zone: Use as an annual for the most color in containers.

Pest problems: None known in my trials.

Use: Accent or side plant in side-planted containers.

Size: The upright variety (which I have had bad luck with) grows about 6"-8" tall. The trailing types grow about 8" down the sides of a container.

Colors: Red, white, purple, and pink.

Average life: 2-6 months as a decorative plant in a container.

Cautions: Unknown

Violas

Violas are similar to pansies, except the flowers are smaller. They do well during the cool times of the year and thrive in shade. Flowers are edible.

Care: Very easy. Plant with slow-release fertilizer described on page 36, and leave them alone!

Water: Medium

Season: Plant when temperatures vary between 22 degrees and the low 80's.

Light: Medium shade to full sun

Zone: Use as an annual.

Pest problems: Occasional aphids or snails.

Use: Mounding plant that works well in the center or along the edges of any pot as well as in the sides of hanging baskets.

Size: 4"-6" tall and equally as wide.

Colors: Lavender, blue, purple, red, brown and yellow.

Average life: Grow for at least 6 months in zones 7-8 in winter. Shorter lifespan farther south. Do well for about 3 months in spring in zones 3-6. Bloom for most of the time they are alive.

Cautions: Unknown

Zinnia

Zinnias come in many sizes. I use the large ones for centerpieces, but they frequently get bad fungus spots on the leaves. The 'Profusion' series is quite small but doesn't get fungus.

Care: Very easy. Plant with slow-release fertilizer described on page 36, and leave them alone!

Water: Medium

Season: Plant when temperatures vary between 45 degrees and the low-100's.

Light: Full sun

Zone: Use as an annual.

Pest problems: Fungus on leaves of all but the 'Profusion' series.

Use: Larger ones, centerpiece. Smaller ones, accent, but not good for sides of side-planted containers.

Size: 6"-5' tall, depending on variety.

Colors: Pink, peach, orange, red, and white.

Average life: One growing season.

Cautions: None known

Plant Profiles: Vegetables

1ST — Arugula

Arugula is sometimes classified as a vegetable because it's eaten in salads; other times, it's classified as an herb since it is also used to give a mustard flavor to other foods. Either way, it's quite easy to grow. I just planted it and left it alone, other than watering. As long as you water it enough and keep it in cool temperatures, it does well. It didn't look great in a container, however, simply because it's not a very attractive plant. Plant with flowers if you want it to look good!

Arugula, also called rocket or roquette, is used in salads and cooked greens. Cooking arugula is as easy as sauteing spinach. You can even add the flowers to a salad for a peppery taste. Home-grown arugula tastes quite a bit better than what you find at your grocery store. It has long been popular in Europe but has recently been introduced in the US. For some good recipes using arugula, go to www.bonnieplants.com.

CHARACTERISTICS

Average Size in a Container: Varies from 8"-15" tall and equally as wide. Flowers shoot upward to 24" tall, but the plant is basically done once the flowers appear, unless you like the leaves to taste quite strong.

Lifespan: 4-7 months

Production: Look at the plant in the container on the opposite page. It shows the minimum amount of arugula you can harvest from one plant. Keep cutting the leaves on the outside, however. This will increase production by stimulating new leaf growth from the center.

VARIETIES TESTED

There are no named varieties or cultivars of arugula.

GROWING CONDITIONS

Light: Full sun, at least 6 hours per day.

Water: Medium. I watered every 2-3 days.

Hardiness: Tolerates temperatures from 30-65 degrees, with optimum temperatures ranging from 40-55 degrees. If a few days are warmer than 65, it really does not matter. I planted mine in September in Georgia, and I still had days in the low 80's. In fall, if the temperature drop is gradual, the plants can adjust to light freezes. Arugula can last all winter in zone 8 and warmer.

1ST   Blue ribbon vegetables are defined on pages 12-13.

Arugula in a container

Arugula and cherry tomatoes on pizza

Propagation: Seeds, but it's easier to buy small plants.

Pest and Diseases: I had no pests on my arugula. Flea beetles sometimes eat it.

CARE & HARVESTING

Planting Day: Follow planting instructions on pages 32-35. Use the fertilizer shown on page 36.

Trimming & Supporting: Be sure to cut the outside leaves first. After the plant flowers, it sometimes grows back completely if you cut it back. No support needed.

Harvesting: The leaves are ready as soon as they reach a useful size, at least 4"-6" long. Leaves taste best when they are dark green and smooth. As with lettuce, cut the outside leaves first, so the plant continues to grow. Flowers (not always produced) are also edible. Be sure to refrigerate the leaves right after picking.

The flavor of the leaves gets much stronger after the flowers appear. Pull the plant up if the flavor is too strong for you, or continue harvesting.

CONTAINER DESIGN TIPS

Container Sizes: As with many cool-season vegetables, arugula can be grown in a smallish pot, about 10" wide and equally as deep.

Use: Centerpiece, but it spreads out somewhat and can be unattractive.

Plant Profiles: Vegetables

Beans

Over 600 different kinds of beans are available, including both bush and vine types. I grew 3 different kinds of beans: pole, runner, and bush. Our bush and pole beans are snap beans; while runner beans produce shell beans. Each behaved differently, but all were really easy - just add water after planting! Bush beans grow like bushes and are fast to produce all their beans quickly. Pole beans are slower to mature but produce more beans in the same space as bush beans. Runner beans are more decorative and produce fewer beans at one time but keep producing all summer. They grow like pole beans.

Above: Pole or bush bean Below: Scarlet runner bean

CHARACTERISTICS

Average Size in a Container: Varies from 3'-5' tall, depending on cultivar. The average, large bush bean grew 3'-4' tall in my large containers (16" wide). The larger the pot, the bigger they grow. Runner beans covered a 5' trellis in a huge pot shown on pages 102-103.

Lifespan: 2-6 months, depending on variety.

Production: Each bush and pole bean container (4 plants per container) produced enough beans for about 10 servings. Our runner beans didn't produce many beans because of high temperatures. Runner beans - in areas with 90 days of 60-85 degrees - should produce equivalent harvests from just one plant.

VARIETIES TESTED

'Scarlet Runner Beans': The most famous of all the runner beans; an heirloom vegetable; bears beautiful, red flowers all summer long but not as many beans as bush and pole beans. Very easy to grow, provided you give it a large, secure support. Expect to take some time to keep this huge vine on its support. It takes runner beans 90 days on average to produce beans.

'Tricolor Bush Beans': One of my favorite vegetables because it is so easy! See pages 46-47 for more information.

'Tricolor Pole Beans': The beans are quite similar to the 3-colored 'Tricolor Bush Beans.' Didn't produce beans as quickly as the bush beans, but produced more. Grows like a vine, so give it big support.

GROWING CONDITIONS

Light: Full sun, at least 6 hours per day. Don't even think of less!

Water: High. I watered daily.

 Blue ribbon vegetables are defined on pages 12-13.

Left: Scarlet runner bean flower Right, top: Purple bush bean flower Right, bottom: White bush bean flower

Hardiness: Don't plant until danger of frost is over. Optimum temperatures are 60-85 degrees, but I grew mine reasonably well at 75-95 degrees. Our pole and bush beans produced lots of beans at these temperatures. The runner beans, which have a reputation for not setting fruit at temperatures over 90 degrees, did not bear many beans, but did produce lots of flowers! Minimum temperature is 50 degrees for pole and bush beans, while runner beans take a light frost.

Propagation: Seeds. I grew my pole and bush beans quite easily from seeds because I couldn't find plants at my garden center. Seeds germinate in only a few days if the temperatures are over 85 degrees, and a few weeks in temperatures as low as 60 degrees. I was lucky enough to find a large runner bean plant at a nursery.

Pest and Diseases: Traditionally, beans have hosted many pests and diseases. However, many new cultivars are resistant. Our pole and bush beans had some spots on the leaves, which I ignored because they weren't severe. The runner beans were pest-free. Mexican bean beetles can sometimes chew leaves.

CARE & HARVESTING

Planting Day: Follow planting instructions on pages 32-35. Use the fertilizer shown on page 36.

Trimming & Supporting: Both pole and runner beans produce huge plants that need large trellises or obelisks to keep them upright. I even put an obelisk around my bush beans because some of the branches started to fall over. Trim the bean plants just to keep them from taking over your garden!

Harvesting: Cut off the beans with scissors to keep from damaging the plant. Runner beans can be har-

vested at 3 different times. Pick when they are flat, and treat them like snap beans. For shell beans, pick when the pods have filled out but before they have changed color. For dried beans, allow the beans to fully mature. Pick bush and pole beans (snap beans) when still young and plump, before the seeds inside the pods have begun to swell and when they are about 1/4" in diameter. Harvest when leaves are dry to discourage pests. Also, runner beans produce more flowers if the bean pods are removed frequently.

CONTAINER DESIGN TIPS

Container Sizes: I used 16" wide pots as a minimum. The larger the better!

Use: Centerpiece. I grew some of my beans alone in attractive containers and hardware. Others, we surrounded with flowers. The beans did equally well in either situation.

Plant Profiles: Vegetables

Broccoli Cool-Season Vegetable

Broccoli is not the easiest vegetable. It requires cool temperatures for longer time periods than most areas have in order to produce the large heads as seen at the grocery store. However, it is quite popular and did well in my trials. Broccoli is easier to grow in containers because it requires rich soil, and the good-quality potting mixes fit the bill well. Early maturing varieties, like 'Early Dividend,' are better choices for warm areas.

CHARACTERISTICS

Average Size in a Container: Depends on variety. I tried only full-size broccoli, which grew about 16" tall by 12" wide.

Lifespan: 2-4 months

Production: Most broccoli plants only produce 1 head, with some small offshoots.

VARIETIES TESTED

'Early Dividend' is the only variety I tested. It did quite well and produced fruit earlier than I expected. Many container gardeners are sticking with dwarf varieties, like 'Munchkin' and 'Small Miracle,' but I have no first-hand experience with those.

GROWING CONDITIONS

Light: Full sun, at least 6 hours per day.

Water: Medium. I watered every 2-3 days.

Hardiness: Broccoli withstands a minimum temperature of 37 and a maximum temperature of 75. Optimum temperature is 60-65 degrees. If plants are exposed to temperatures under 40 degrees for more than a week, the heads form too early and won't do well. The same thing happens if you plant too late. Check with your local county extension (find their number at www.csrees.usda.gov) to find the ideal planting dates for your area. Be sure to take it inside if a freeze threatens.

Propagation: Seeds, but it's easier to buy small plants.

Pest and Diseases: I didn't get any pests in my trials, probably because broccoli growing in containers gets fewer pests than if grown in the ground. Common pests include flea beetles, cabbage loopers and other caterpillars, and aphids.

CARE & HARVESTING

Planting Day: Follow planting instructions on pages 32-35. Use the fertilizer shown on page 36.

Trimming & Supporting: None required, other than harvesting.

Harvesting: Cut off the head while the buds are still tight and green. If you should see any yellow, tiny flowers appearing cut the head anyway, even if it is small. Past this point, it won't be any good. The head grows out of the middle of the plant, from the top. This first head is the main one the plant will produce, but it will sometimes produce smaller, bite-sized heads where the leaves join the stalk. If you harvest these side shoots every few days, more will grow. Don't expect your broccoli heads to be as large as the ones you buy at the grocery because these are grown in ideal temperatures that are only found in a few areas of the country.

CONTAINER DESIGN TIPS

Container Sizes: Like most cool-season vegetables, broccoli does well in medium-sized containers. For full-sized plants, use pots at least 10" in diameter and equally as deep.

Use: Centerpiece only. I tried it in the side holes of side-planted baskets, and it really looked weird! Broccoli has a tendency to get leggy in containers, so underplant with flowers as shown on pages 60-61.

146   EASY CONTAINER COMBOS:
       VEGETABLES AND FLOWERS

Brussels sprouts need cool weather for quite a while to grow as large as the ones you see in the grocery store. They are known to thrive in the Pacific Northwest, in an area known as the fog belt.

Left: Brussel sprouts   *Right: They grow along the stem of the plant.*

CHARACTERISTICS

Average Size in a Container: 18" tall and 9" wide for the 'Bubbles' that I tried. Taller Brussels sprouts exist.

Lifespan: 2-7 months

Production: One plant bears about 50 sprouts.

VARIETIES TESTED

'Bubbles': The only one I tried. More tolerant of warm weather than many others and also gets few pests.

GROWING CONDITIONS

Light: Full sun, at least 6 hours per day. Don't even think of less!

Water: High. I watered daily in warm weather and every 3 days in cooler temperatures.

Hardiness: Tolerates temperatures ranging from 28-75 degrees, with optimum temperatures ranging from 60-65 degrees. Plant in spring in cooler climates and in fall in warmer locations. Brussels sprouts don't do well in zones 9-10 because those areas aren't cold enough. Don't make the mistake I did of planting them in spring in Georgia, when there is not enough cool weather for them to mature. If they mature in hot weather, they taste awful! Check with your local county extension (see www.csrees.usda.gov) to find the ideal varieties and planting date for your area.

Propagation: Seeds, but it's easier to buy small plants.

Pest and Diseases: Our Brussels sprouts (the ones I planted in the correct season!) didn't get any pests, possibly because container vegetables get fewer pests than those grown in the ground. Common pests include aphids, which can be hard to control, and flea beetles. Many other pests are common. Look for varieties that are resistant.

CARE & HARVESTING

Planting Day: Plant shortly after buying the plants. Follow planting instructions on pages 32-35, but be aware that many people plant Brussels sprouts deeply, so only about 1/3 of the plant is out of the soil. I planted mine level (or even a bit above the soil line), and they did just fine. Use the fertilizer shown on page 36. This fertilizer is particularly well-suited to Brussels sprouts because it includes boron, which they require. Do not use a fertilizer without boron on Brussels sprouts.

Trimming & Supporting: None required.

Harvesting: Look for the sprouts forming along the stalk of the plant. They start forming at the bottom of the plant and keep forming and moving towards the top. Twist them away from the plant when they are 1/2"-2" in diameter. They are past their prime if they start to open. Place unwashed sprouts in plastic bags in the refrigerator.

CONTAINER DESIGN TIPS

Container Sizes: Like most cool-season vegetables, Brussels sprouts do well in medium-sized containers. For full-sized plants, use pots at least 10" in diameter and equally as deep.

Use: Centerpiece only. I tried it in the side holes of side-planted baskets, and it really looked weird! Brussels sprouts have a tendency to get leggy in containers, so underplant with flowers as shown on page 72.

Plant Profiles: Vegetables

Cabbage and Kale

Cabbage and kale are related, and both come in an amazing array of types and sizes. Some are edible, and some are just grown for their attractive appearance, not their taste. All of them did well for us in containers, although some of the cabbages ended up with splotches as well as a few holes in the leaves. Because of their pest vulnerability, they don't rate a ribbon. Cabbages come in a variety of shapes (flat, round, pointed, head-shaped) as well as different colors - green, blue-green, and red (the red looks more purple to me). Leaves are smooth or wrinkled.

Kale is not anywhere near as susceptible to pests as cabbages, and they live longer in containers, so they are a better container plant. I would probably have given them a blue ribbon if I had more experience with them. They also come in a variety of leaf shapes and textures. Some taste wonderful, and some, called ornamental kale, are used primarily for garnish. Ornamentals with rounded forms and leaves are commonly called ornamental cabbages, and ornamentals with fringed or feathery leaves are called ornamental kale

'Bonnie Hybrid' cabbage in a 'Beehive' container in copper from www.anamese.com. The container measures 15"W x 15"H.

CHARACTERISTICS

Average Size in a Container: See 'Varieties Tested,' below.

Lifespan: 2-5 months

Production: One cabbage plant bears one head. Each kale plant produces about 15-30 leaves.

VARIETIES TESTED

'Ruby Red Perfection' Cabbage: Medium-sized head, about 6" tall and wide in containers; did well in side holes. See photo #3 at far right. The cabbages look purple to me!

'Savoy' Cabbage: Larger than red cabbage, growing to about 12" tall and wide in containers. Attractive, krinkly leaves. Also did well in side holes. The most cold-hardy cabbage I tried.

Bonnie Hybrid: Largest I tried. Did well planted in 15" container, and grew about 18" tall and wide (shown, left).

Ornamental Cabbage: Used frequently throughout this book. Use for garnish, but doesn't taste good. Grows slowly to about 10" tall and wide. Photo #2 at right.

'Redbor' Kale: Great centerpiece plant. Grows about 24" tall and wide. Edible. Photo #1 at right.

GROWING CONDITIONS

Light: Both cabbage and kale prefer full sun in cool weather and shade in warmer weather.

Water: High. I watered daily in warmer weather and every 2-3 days when it was cooler. Neither cabbage nor kale likes to dry out.

Hardiness: Prefer temperatures between 60-65 degrees, but handle temperatures ranging from 37-75 degrees. Cabbage

Blue ribbon vegetables are defined on pages 12-13.

1. *Redbor kale (edible), violas, and lettuce in 30", side-planted, window box. 2. Ornamental cabbages with Juncus grass and pansies in 24", side-planted, window box. 3. Red cabbage in side holes with a mustard green and pansies in 16", side-planted basket.*

and kale can be grown almost anywhere in the US in zones 2 and warmer. And, timing is the key to success. The heads and leaves need to develop in cool weather. Most southerners grow cabbage and kale in the winter, while northerners plant them in spring or fall. Cabbages and kale can withstand some frost, especially older ones. Check with your local county extension (find their number at www.csrees.usda.gov) to find the ideal varieties and planting date for your area.

Propagation: Seeds, but it's easier to buy small plants.

Pest and Diseases: Flea beetles sometimes feast on young cabbages. Cabbage caterpillars are the worst pests, attacking green but not red ones. Kale gets fewer pests but look for occasional aphids and flea beatles.

CARE & HARVESTING

Planting Day: Follow planting instructions on pages 32-35. Cabbages are one of the few plants that can take having about half of their stem buried. I planted mine at or a little above the soil level, and they did quite well. Use the fertilizer shown on page 36.

Trimming & Supporting: None needed.

Harvesting: Cut the heads of cabbages with a sharp knife at soil level as soon as they feel firm, even if they are only about 5" in diameter. Leave the roots, bottom leaves, and part of the stem, so sprouts or small cabbage heads can develop.

Kale is completely different because the leaves are picked individually. Begin picking when they are only about 3" long. Start from the outside and use a sharp knife to cut the leaf at the base. Cool the

leaves immediately after cutting.

CONTAINER DESIGN TIPS

Container Sizes: The largest cabbage I tried was the 'Bonnie Hybrid.' I planted 3 in the rust-colored pot shown on the opposite page. It measures 15"W x 15"H. Cabbages also work well planted in the side holes of side-planted containers, but I only tried the medium-sized cabbages there.

Use: I planted the largest cabbages by themselves in a pot. Large kale are extremely useful as centerpieces in mixed containers. Medium and small cabbages, along with ornamentals, are very versatile and useful - primarily along the edge or planted in the side holes of a side-planted basket. Occasionally, I used ornamental cabbages as centerpieces, but they stay lower than the ideal centerpiece.

Plant Profiles: Vegetables

Chard, Swiss

Although Swiss chard is classified as the most beautiful of all greens, I was a little disappointed by its appearance in my containers, as shown in the red pot below. Maybe I was expecting too much because I had heard so many reports on how lovely they were! Alone, they looked a little thin. If I tried underplanting with smaller plants, the stems, which are gorgeous, were covered up, but the plants themselves were rather gawky. However, the advantage of growing Swiss chard is that, while it is quite easy to grow, but quite difficult to buy, the leaves taste pretty good, a lot like spinach. Swiss chard offers the additional benefit of being one of the most nutritious vegetables. The plants are also one of the few that tolerate both cool and warm weather, although mine did much better in cooler temperatures. So, grow this plant to cook rather than to create a gorgeous container garden! It is either cooked like spinach or chopped into salads.

Left: Lovely Swiss chard stems

Right: I was a little disappointed in the look of this container.

appear, remove them to prolong the harvest. The outer leaves fall over, so trim these off when or before they fall. Sometimes the whole plant seemed unsteady, so I staked those loosely.

Harvesting: Swiss chard matures quickly and can be harvested for many months. The leaves taste best in cool, not hot or cold, weather. Break off the outer leaves at their base anytime since they have a tendency to fall over anyway. The new, tender leaves growing out of the middle of the plant taste the best. Be sure to remove the midrib of larger leaves before cooking or using in a salad. Put whole leaves in a plastic bag in the refrigerator, where they live for about 2 weeks.

CONTAINER DESIGN TIPS

Container Sizes: Like most cool-season vegetables, Swiss chard do well in medium-sized containers. For full-sized plants, use pots at least 10" in diameter and equally as deep.

Use: Swiss chard looks best alone so the stems show easily. Plant several in the same pot.

Swiss chard planted as a centerpiece and surrounded by lettuce. The lettuce contrasts well with the dark color of the chard leaves, but the gorgeous stems are mostly covered.

CHARACTERISTICS

Average Size in a Container: About 18"-24" tall by equally as wide.

Lifespan: 2-7 months

Production: One plant bears about 12-18 leaves.

VARIETIES TESTED

'Bright Lights': This is the only variety I tried; wildly popular.

GROWING CONDITIONS

Light: Does best in full sun, but lives on a minimum of 4 hours of sun per day. Likes more sun in cool weather and less in heat.

Water: Medium. I watered every 2-3 days in cool weather but every day in hot weather.

Hardiness: Much more tolerant of different temperature ranges than most leafy vegetables. Tolerates 40-90 degrees, but prefers 50-85 degrees. Plants die in a hard freeze.

Propagation: Seeds, but it's easier to buy small plants.

Pest and Diseases: Plants generally don't attract many pests in containers except for slugs, but leaves can occasionally be chewed by caterpillars. For more information about pests, see www.bonnieplants.com.

CARE & HARVESTING

Planting Day: Follow planting instructions on pages 32-35. Use the fertilizer shown on page 36.

Trimming & Supporting: If flowers

Collards

Although collards have traditionally been used in southern cooking, their popularity is rapidly spreading because of their high nutritional value. Collards provide more nutrients than any other vegetable! Luckily, collards grow well throughout the country, tolerating cold better than most other vegetables. These healthy vegetables earn a blue ribbon because they are so easy to grow. For some great collard recipes and a little southern food culture, see www.bonnieplants.com.

CHARACTERISTICS

Average Size in a Container: About 18"-24" tall by equally as wide.

Lifespan: 2-12 months because spring-planted collards will make it through summer, fall, and winter in zones 7b and warmer, until they flower the following spring.

Production: Each plant produces about 50 leaves.

VARIETIES TESTED

'Top Bunch': The only variety I tested. Known for heavy yields and early maturity.

GROWING CONDITIONS

Light: Prefer full sun, at least 6 hours per day, but will tolerate 4-5 hours per day.

Water: High. I watered daily in warmer temperatures and every 2-3 days when it got cooler.

Hardiness: Collards are tolerant to moderate heat and cold, from 22-80 degrees. In warm areas, plant collards in early fall. In zones 8 and south, they live all winter. In cooler areas, plant collards in spring for a fall harvest. Collards taste better after a frost. The optimum temperature for growing collards is 60-65 degrees.

Propagation: Seeds, but it's easier to buy small plants.

Pest and Diseases: Collards are similar to kale in their pest susceptibility. See page 149 for details.

CARE & HARVESTING

Planting Day: Follow planting instructions on pages 32-35. Collards can also be planted with the stem half-buried, but I planted mine as shown on pages 32-35. Use the fertilizer shown on page 36.

Trimming & Supporting: None needed.

Harvesting: Collards can be harvested almost from the moment they have their first leaves until they are quite mature. You can cut off the leaves as soon as they are large enough to use (about 10" long) and continue picking from time to time throughout the plants' lifespan. Be sure to pick the oldest, outside leaves first, so the plant can keep growing out of the middle. Or, the whole plant can be taken out of the ground and cooked at almost any point in its development. Wash the leaves and put them in cool water promptly after picking.

CONTAINER DESIGN TIPS

Container Sizes: Use a container at least 14" wide by 12" deep. Collards look rather plain alone, so plant flowers around the base. Pansies or violas work well.

Use: Centerpiece only

Collards look best surrounded by flowers. This collard centerpiece is surrounded by purple violas and pink petunias. The container is a 16" side-planted basket on an ornate patio stand. See page 6 for sources.

Plant Profiles: Vegetables

Cucumbers

2ND

Cucumbers are not only one of the most popular vegetables but also very easy to grow in containers in areas with low humidity. However, I grew them in Georgia in high humidity and had a successful crop. This easy crop, planted in April, bore a lot of fruit with very little care. My luck didn't hold for the cucumber plants I planted later - they died from downy mildew, mainly because I didn't spray properly when the heat and humidity had increased the risk. See page 43 to learn correct spraying methods. Be aware that not all parts of the country have problems with downy mildew.

Like beans, cucumbers come in either bush or vine form. Most container gardeners use the bushes because they take up only about one third as much space. I couldn't find the bush type, however, so I grew the vines, which produce more fruit. Since I grew them up trellises, they didn't require that much more ground space.

Cucumbers grow only in very warm weather and don't do well north of zone 4. There are 2 main types: picklers and slicers. Picklers bear fruit earlier but produce for a much shorter time period. Picklers also bear fruit for only about 10 days while slicers continue for 4-6 weeks.

CHARACTERISTICS

Average Size in a Container: Large, vine cucumbers completely cover trellises that are 5' tall. Bush cucumbers are quite a bit shorter.

Lifespan: 3-4 months

Production: Our large vines produced about 30 large cucumbers each when planted in large pots. As side plants in side-planted containers, each plant produced about 16 fruit that were much smaller but tasted great. I didn't try the bush types.

VARIETIES TESTED

Unknown: The cucumber I tested had no name on the label.

GROWING CONDITIONS

Light: Full sun, at least 6 hours per day. Don't even think of less!

Water: High. Cucumbers are mainly water. I watered daily. Lack of water produces bitter fruit with weird shapes. If possible, water the soil and not the leaves to inhibit disease.

Hardiness: Cucumbers like warm weather with a minimum temperature of 60 degrees and maximum of 90 degrees. Check with your local county extension (find their number at www.csrees.usda.gov) to find the ideal varieties and planting date for your area.

Propagation: Seeds, but it's easier to buy small plants.

Pest and Diseases: Cucumbers grown vertically (up trellises or other supports) have better air circulation and attract fewer pests. Also, cucumbers grown in containers are less susceptible to diseases than those grown in the ground.

Downy mildew was the worst pest I encountered, but it doesn't appear in dry areas of the coun-

 Blue ribbon vegetables are defined on pages 12-13.

pick, the more your plant will produce.

CONTAINER DESIGN TIPS

Container Sizes: I grew large cucumbers in both side-planted baskets and traditional containers. The large, vining types did surprisingly well in the side-holes of baskets as small as 16" wide. The fruit were smaller, about 3"-4" long, but quite good, and production was excellent. See pages116-117 for an example.

I used very large (20" wide) traditional containers with large trellises. The production was huge! If you use a traditional container, be sure to find one that can easily include a trellis. Check out the square one I used on pages 94-95. Square containers fit trellises well. Don't make the mistake I did of putting the trellis in after the cucumber had started to grow quite large! It is rather difficult to do, so put your trellis in place on planting day.

Use: Centerpiece growing up a trellis or side plant in a side-planted container.

Cucumber often grow under the leaves, where they are hard to see. I missed harvesting quite a few because I didn't know they were there!

try. Be sure that any pesticide you use doesn't kill bees because cucumbers need pollination from bees.

CARE & HARVESTING

Planting Day: Follow planting instructions on pages 32-35. Use the fertilizer shown on page 36.

Trimming & Supporting: Cucumbers grown vertically (up trellises or other supports) have much larger yields. I used decorative trellises to support them. Place the trellis in the container prior to planting. As the vines grow, attach them loosely to the trellis.

Harvesting: Cut off the fruit with scissors to keep from damaging the vine. Cucumbers grow incredibly fast and often cannot be easily seen behind the leaves. Check the plants often, or you will miss them, like I did.

Cucumbers taste best when they are medium-sized, no larger than 6"-8" long for slicers grown in large pots, or 3"-4" long for picklers. Pick them when they are smaller, if you are growing them in smaller pots and they seem to have stopped growing. If left on the vine too long, they become bitter. They also don't taste great when they are too young. Keep harvesting as they ripen because the more you

Cucumber flower

Plant Profiles: Vegetables

Eggplant

2ND

Warm-Season Vegetable

Eggplants are the most beautiful vegetables and are now available in a wide variety of colors, shapes, and sizes. The fruit comes in many shades of pink, purple, yellow, or white and are preceded by lovely flowers. Fruits vary in shape from short and fat to long and skinny, but all of them taste about the same. Eggplants are easier to grow in containers than in the ground but need warm (hot is better!) temperatures - some parts of the country are too cold for them. Another advantage of eggplant is the appearance of the plant - it looks much better than many other vegetables.

your area (and when to plant them) is to check with the local county extension (find their number at www.csrees.usda.gov). Extension offices can also provide you with a list of varieties that do well in your area, which is important information. Some varieties (like 'Orient Express') produce fruit fairly quickly, in about 60 days from seed, while others take 100 days. You need the faster varieties in colder climates.

Propagation: Buy small plants because seeds take too long in most climates.

Pest and Diseases: Flea beetles eat little holes in the leaves, which I ignored. See page 42 for more information.

CARE & HARVESTING

Planting Day: Follow planting instructions on pages 32-35. Use the fertilizer shown on page 36.

Trimming & Supporting: Branches need staking when the fruit weighs them down.

Harvesting: Cut off the fruit with scissors to keep from damaging the plant, leaving about 1" of stem on the fruit. Timing is important because it tastes bitter if underripe or overripe. Wait until the fruit has stopped growing and has a glossy skin. Frequent harvesting stimulates more fruit production.

CONTAINER DESIGN TIPS

Container Sizes: The smallest traditional container I tried was quite large, about 20" wide. The 'Ichiban' did well planted in the side holes of side-planted baskets.

Use: Centerpiece or plant smaller varieties in the side holes of side-planted baskets.

Other Tips: I was able to crowd flowers around them and still get quite a bit of fruit if I let the plant grow alone for a few weeks first.

CHARACTERISTICS

Average Size in a Container: Varies from 1'-4' tall, depending on cultivar. The average, large plant grew 3'-4' tall in my large containers (20" wide by equally as tall). The larger the pot, the bigger they grow. The 'Ichiban' eggplant grew 3' tall in a huge pot and only about 1' tall when planted in the side holes of a side-planted basket.

Lifespan: 3-6 months

Production: My large eggplant produced 20 pounds of fruit all at once - it would have produced more had I harvested more often (see photos on pages 34-35). The 'Ichiban' variety produced about 10 fruit per plant in traditional containers and 4 fruit per plant in the side holes of side-planted baskets.

VARIETIES TESTED

Unknown: I tried one, large plant that had no variety name. It is pictured on pages 34-35.

'Ichiban:' Smaller plants with long, thin fruit. The plants bear an amazing amount of fruit.

GROWING CONDITIONS

Light: Full sun, at least 6 hours per day. Don't even think of less!

Water: High. I watered daily. Lack of water produces small, bitter fruit.

Hardiness: Tolerates temperatures from 50-95 degrees, with optimum temperatures ranging from 70-85. Needs 100-140 days of temperatures between 70-90 degrees. All eggplants are damaged at temperatures under 50 degrees and will stop producing when the nights start to get too cool in fall. The easiest way to find out whether they grow in

 Blue ribbon vegetables are defined on pages 12-13.

1ST

'Greens' include lots of leafy vegetables, such as lettuce, chard, collard, and kale, plus mustard and turnip greens. All but mustard and turnip greens are covered in their own plant profiles, so this page is limited to mustard and turnip greens. There are many mustard greens - so many that it is hard to keep them straight. But, both mustard and turnip greens are easy, fast, and grown in zone 2 south. While some mustard varieties are grown for seeds, most container gardeners prefer those grown for their leaves. Mustard greens are one of my favorite centerpieces for cool-season combos. Most are used either in salads or cooked.

accurate information about planting dates in your area is to go to your county extension. Find the number at www.csrees.usda.gov.

Propagation: Seeds, but easier to buy small plants.

Pest and Diseases: Watch for aphids and mites.

CARE & HARVESTING

Planting Day: Follow planting instructions on pages 32-35. Use the fertilizer shown on page 36.

Trimming & Supporting: Remove older, yellow leaves as they appear.

Harvesting: Cut off the leaves with scissors to keep from damaging the plant. Harvest greens whenever you wish! Turnip greens will grow more leaves with each picking until the first hard frost and sometimes beyond. The leaves taste best when the temperatures are in the 40's or cooler. Cut turnip greens back about 2" above the root and they quickly sprout more leaves. Wash the leaves thoroughly because they often have soil bits on them. Either cook them immediately or place them in a plastic bag in a refrigerator for a few days. Freeze or steam them later

Left: Mustard greens, which also come in lime green.   Right: Turnip greens

CHARACTERISTICS

Average Size in a Container: Mustard greens vary from 1'-3' tall and equally as wide. The larger the pot, the bigger they grow. I was able to crowd flowers around them and still get quite a bit of height from the plant.

Turnip greens are much smaller, growing 8"-12" tall in medium-sized (about 10"-14" wide) containers.

Lifespan: 3-7 months

Production: A lot of leaves! I did not count how many I harvested, but each plant creates quite a bit, particularly if you harvest the side leaves, which encourages more new leaves from the center.

VARIETIES TESTED

Unknown: All the plants I tried simply said 'mustard greens' or

'turnip greens' on the label.

GROWING CONDITIONS

Light: Grows fastest in full sun, but tolerates only 4-5 hours of sun per day.

Water: High. I watered daily when temperatures were warm and every other day in cooler weather. Mustard greens wilt when they need water and other times when they just feel too much sun. Check the potting mix to see if it is moist before watering. If it is moist and the mustard greens are just hot, you don't need to give it additional water. They will recover quickly.

Hardiness: Tolerate temperatures from 37-80 degrees, with optimum temperatures ranging from 60-65 degrees. Plants thrive in cool weather; plant them in cooler areas in spring and plant in fall in hotter places. The leaves taste better after a frost. The easiest way to get the most

CONTAINER DESIGN TIPS

Container Sizes: I used mustard greens solely as centerpieces in containers as small as 14" wide up to 28" wide. They got much larger in bigger pots. I only tried turnip greens once, in a 14" diameter pot.

Use: Centerpiece

Other Tips: The turnip root can be cooked with the greens if you cut away the skin and any blemishes. Cut the rest into cubes prior to cooking. Turnip roots generally do better planted in the ground than in containers.

Plant Profiles: Vegetables

Lettuce

1ST

I heard that lettuce is one of the easiest plants to grow in containers - so easy that many vegetable growers no longer grow it in the ground. But, I kept thinking it was dying after my first plantings because it would wilt every day, even right after I watered it! I quickly realized that this is normal behavior with lettuce, particularly when the sun hits it. If it wilts and the potting mix is wet, don't water it again that day. It will recover on its own in a little while.

It took some practice to get it to look good in containers. My first idea was to mix quite a few different lettuces together and call it the 'salad bowl.' I tried it in a bowl, and it looked awful - probably because the leaves were a little different but not enough to be able to clearly see the difference. My next attempt was in a strawberry pot, which looked better (photo, opposite) but a little weird as well. These attempts taught me two important design guidelines with lettuce. First, keep it simple. It's easiest to limit the number of different lettuces to two in one pot for fast, easy designing (example, below). Second, if you want lots of different lettuce in one pot, look for 'mixed lettuce,' which is lots of different kinds of lettuce seeds grown in the same pots by growers. It's sometimes hard to find, so don't hesitate to buy some if you find it at a garden center. See it planted in a window box on page 127.

There are two basic forms of lettuce: leaf lettuce and head lettuce, with many variations of the two. Head lettuce forms like a head of cabbage, while leaf lettuce forms a loose clump. I like leaf lettuce the best because it is the easiest one to grow, fastest to mature, and most flexible, allowing you to pick several leaves at a time without taking out the whole plant. Leaf lettuce also looks terrific in containers, either around the edge of a centerpiece or planted in the holes of side-planted containers. 'Butterhead' is in between a tight-headed lettuce and leaf lettuce. It is considered the best tasting.

Simplicity works best with lettuce. This combo features rosemary in the center, with 'Red Velvet' and 'Simpson Elite' lettuce alternated around the edge.

CHARACTERISTICS

Average Size in a Container: See 'Varieties Tested' below.

Lifespan: 2-4 months

Production: Varies by type

VARIETIES TESTED

'Buttercrunch': Hardiest lettuce that makes an attractive rosette. Grows about 6"-8" tall by equally as wide. More heat-tolerant than most, too. A bibb lettuce.

'Iceburg': Forms nice, tight heads only in locations that have a long, cool period, like California. Can be used elsewhere and still tastes good, but doesn't develop a tight head. Grows about 6" tall and equally as wide.

'Red' or 'Red Sails': One of the prettiest lettuces I tried. Frilly and loose. A leaf lettuce. Red color appears as the weather cools. About 8" tall and wide.

'Romaine': Don't plant this one if it looks leggy in the nursery pot. Taller than most, growing about 12" tall and 8" wide. Not as attractive in a pot as many other lettuces, but has a distinctive taste. A bit gawky. This is the Caesar salad lettuce.

'Mascara': Reddish-brown lettuce I used extensively. Grows about 6" tall by equally as wide. Really attractive and fast-growing. See it in containers on page 23.

'Red Velvet': Great container plant. Grows about 6" tall by equally as wide. Looks good alternated with 'Simpson Elite.' See pages 50, 70, and 125.

'Simpson Elite': Love the lime-green color of this lettuce. Grows about 6" tall by equally as wide. I alternated it frequently with 'Red Velvet.' See pages 50, 70, and 125.

Mixed Lettuce: This is my favorite. Growers sow different

Blue ribbon vegetables are defined on pages 12-13.

Ornamental kale planted in the center with 4 different lettuces in the sides.

CARE & HARVESTING

Planting Day: Follow planting instructions on pages 32-35. Use the fertilizer shown on page 36.

Trimming & Supporting: None needed.

Harvesting: Cut off the outer leaves of leaf and romaine lettuce, leaving the center to grow more leaves. Or, you can cut off the whole plant at the bottom, but it won't grow back. I prefer the leaf-by-leaf method; that way, my container garden lasts longer. Leaf lettuce is ready at any time.

Bibb lettuce (like 'Buttercrunch,' that forms a loose clump) can be harvested at any time (leaf by leaf if you like) but most people wait until the plant has formed its classic rosette. Same for iceberg. But, in warmer climates where head lettuce might not form a tight head, you can harvest them leaf by leaf like leaf lettuce.

Any lettuce is best picked in the morning.

Lettuce tastes best in cool weather. It you see a flower stalk growing out of the center, it's done and is too bitter for most people. However, if you see the stalk forming, remove all the lettuce and put it in the refrigerator. One taste will tell you if you got it in time!

CONTAINER DESIGN TIPS

Container Sizes: Lettuce takes crowding well. You can grow quite a bit in a small bowl because its roots don't require much space. Check out the small bowl on the opposite page. It measures 16" wide but only 7" deep. That combo lasted for 4 months! Not too many other vegetables would last so long in such a small pot.

Use: Edge plant or plant in the side holes of a side-planted basket.

kinds of lettuce seeds into the same pot. Grows about 6" tall by equally as wide. See the results on page 127.

GROWING CONDITIONS

Light: Grows best in full sun, but tolerates some shade. Don't give it less than 4-5 hours per day of sun. Lettuce particularly appreciates shading from the afternoon sun on warm days. The red lettuce needs sun to develop its full color.

Water: High. I watered daily in warm weather and every other day as it cooled off. Never let the soil dry out or the leaves will become bitter. Water in the daytime to discourage leaf diseases.

Hardiness: Grows in most areas in the mild temperatures of spring and fall, best in temperatures between 45 to about 80 degrees. Optimum temperatures range from 60-65 degrees. Don't attempt it in hot weather or it will taste bitter. Some types of bibb lettuce, like 'Buttercrunch' will take some frost if well-rooted. Protect other varieties if the temperatures dip into the low 30's.

The easiest way to find out whether they grow in your area (and when to plant them) is to check with your local county extension (find their number at www.csrees.usda.gov). Most extension offices can also provide you with a list of varieties that do well in your area.

Propagation: Seeds, but it's easier to buy small plants.

Pest and Diseases: Aphids are the most common pest. I had none, but I did spot some white flies. There weren't many and they disappeared without doing significant damage.

Plant Profiles: Vegetables

Okra

Warm-Season Vegetable

2ND

Okra is easy to grow and is attractive, but it is only grown in areas that have long, warm periods. They grow primarily in areas south of and including zone 4, but they are much easier in the hot weather (above 85 degrees for 2 months). Okra has traditionally been used more in the south, but people in other regions are discovering its unique taste, particularly when used in soups or stews. Okra can also be fried or simply boiled. It's easy to grow and one of the easiest vegetables I tried! I did nothing at all after planting other than add water. The only big mistake I made was not understanding how quickly the pods formed. They hide under the leaves and appear overnight. Since they taste best when picked small (3"-4" long), you need to really check under the leaves of the plant frequently (every day), so you don't miss your harvest!

CHARACTERISTICS

Average Size in a Container: Mine grew about 4' tall by 3' wide.

Lifespan: 3-4 months

Production: If you harvest frequently, expect about 50 okra from one large plant.

VARIETIES TESTED

'Clemson Spineless': The only one I tested.

GROWING CONDITIONS

Light: Full sun, at least 6 hours per day. Don't even think of less!

Water: Okra is known for being more drought-tolerant than most vegetables. Since I had the okra on the same drip watering system as the other vegetables, it received the same amount of water as all the other vegetables and did quite well with it. I watered daily.

Hardiness: Tolerates temperatures from 65-95 degrees, with optimum temperatures ranging from 75-90 degrees. Most okra need 70 days of warmth to produce fruit, but new varieties are popping up for cooler areas. The easiest way to find out whether they grow in your area and when to plant them is to check with your local county extension (find their number at www.csrees.usda.gov). Most extension offices can also provide you with a list of varieties that do well in your area. I got my plants in early May in Georgia. They grew slowly until the temperatures rose above 85; after that, they grew unbelievably fast. Pods appear in only 2 months of hot weather, so northerners often wait until late June to

plant.

Propagation: Seeds, but it's easier to buy small plants.

Pest and Diseases: Not too many pests hit okra routinely. I had none on mine. Some pests that show up occasionally include Japanese beetles, aphids, and flea beetles.

CARE & HARVESTING

Planting Day: Follow planting instructions on pages 32-35. Use the fertilizer shown on page 36. Small okra plants have taproots that can't be broken, so water them prior to planting and treat them gently.

Trimming & Supporting: In really hot climates, some gardeners cut back about 1/3 of the plant in late summer, which encourages growth of another crop.

Harvesting: Cut off the fruit with scissors to keep from damaging the vine; leave a stub of stem attached. Harvest frequently to encourage the growth of more okra. Check plants daily for fruit when the weather gets hot. They grow so quickly that it is easy to miss them, like I did. Okra that are too large don't taste good, so pick them when they are 2"-4" long. If you have some that are too large, remove them from the plant to encourage more fruit production. Protect your skin with long sleeves and gloves because some people get a rash from leaf contact.

CONTAINER DESIGN TIPS

Container Sizes: Large! Use a container with a minimum diameter of 16" or has a soil capacity for 10 gallons of potting mix.

Use: Okra look good alone in a pot, as shown on page 53. They also do well as a centerpiece surrounded by flowers, as shown on page 31.

 Blue ribbon vegetables are defined on pages 12-13.

More than 200 cultivars of peas are on the market today. They are grown in almost all areas of the US, from zone 2 south. The main categories of peas are garden peas (the ones you buy in the can), snow peas (can eat both pod and peas), and snap peas, which are a cross between the two. I tested only the sugar snap, because it is the most popular and versatile pea. You can eat it, pod and all, if it's small, or harvest the peas out of the pod if it's larger. Peas are not my favorite vegetable to grow for 2 reasons. First, it takes a lot of plants to produce just a few peas. Second, training them up a trellis takes more time than I want to invest in one vegetable.

CHARACTERISTICS

Average Size in a Container: Varies from 1'-6' tall. My only experience with peas in containers is the 2' tall 'Sugar Ann Snap.' I have heard that some of the other, really big ones might be difficult to support in a container/trellis combination.

Lifespan: 2-5 months, or as long at the temperatures stay from the mid 30's to 80 degrees.

Production: Each plant only produces a handful of peas, so plan on planting quite a few pea plants, close together (3" apart) in a large pot.

VARIETIES TESTED

'Sugar Ann Snap': Only one tested

GROWING CONDITIONS

Light: Full sun, at least 6 hours per day. Don't even think of less!

Water: I watered every 2-4 days, with more in warmer weather. Peas do better if watered early, so the leaves aren't wet at night.

Hardiness: Plants keep producing when the temperatures range from the mid 30's to 80 degrees as long as the soil is cool. Optimum temperatures range from 60-75 degrees.

Propagation: Seeds, but it's easier to buy small plants.

Pest and Diseases: Most peas grown in containers don't get many pests. Birds can eat them, but they are less likely to feast on peas in containers.

CARE & HARVESTING

Planting Day: Follow planting instructions on pages 32-35. Use the fertilizer shown on page 36 strictly according to directions. Too much nitrogen can inhibit pea production, so don't over-fertilize. Be sure to install the trellis the same day you plant, and make sure the trellis is large enough to support the type of pea you are planting.

Trimming & Supporting: Smaller peas, like the 'Sugar Ann Snap' I tested, can be grown without a trellis because they only grow 2' tall. But, it is easier if you trellis them, along with all the larger peas. The vines don't climb the trellis naturally. It takes some fiddling to get the delicate, little branches attached.

Harvesting: Cut off the fruit with scissors to keep from damaging the vine. Harvest frequently (when vines are dry) to encourage more production. Different kinds of peas are harvested at different times. Garden peas are used strictly for the peas inside the pods, like the ones you find canned at the grocery store. Check the pods frequently. When the peas feel plump, open the pod and taste them. If they taste right, harvest the rest that look the same. Sugar snap peas can be harvested the same way, or, if you harvest earlier (when the pods snap like a snap bean), you can eat the whole pod, like snow peas. If harvested later, shell the peas, and eat just the peas. Peas taste best if picked early in the morning, refrigerated promptly, and prepared and eaten shortly thereafter.

CONTAINER DESIGN TIPS

Container Sizes: Peas will grow in smaller containers than most vegetables. Just be sure to plant them close together, about 3" apart.

Use: Centerpiece. Pea plants only grow a few inches wide, so they look better with flowers planted in front of them.

Plant Profiles: Vegetables

Peppers

Peppers are the best vegetable I tried based on a combination of ease of care and high production. All I did was plant them according to the instruction on pages 32-35 and just watered. That's it! No pests, no trimming, nothing at all! I got tons of peppers in the bargain on plants that kept producing from June to November!

They come in all different sizes, shapes, and colors on plants that vary from 1'-6' tall. The only mistake I made was planting the medium-sized plants (about 2' tall by 1.5' wide) in containers that were too small. See 'Container Sizes,' opposite, for the correct sizes.

Sweet, bite-sized bell peppers

smaller than the other bells, but each plant produces much more than any other bell pepper in my trials. Medium-sized plant, about 3' tall by 1.5' wide in a large container. Expect at least 50 fruit from each plant! Intended as finger food. Matures yellow to orange. Is sweetest when orange.

'Big Bertha': Huge, green bell pepper that grows up to 4' tall by 2' wide in large containers. Produced about 14 large, oversized peppers per plant.

'Habanero': Biggest producer of my hot peppers, with 236 produced in one pot of 4 plants! See pages 26-27 for more information. Grew about 2' tall by 1.5' wide in a large container.

'Red Jalapeno': Another hot pepper that grows from about 2' tall by 1.5' wide in a large container. Produced about 50 fruit per plant.

'Red Hot Cherry': Another hot pepper that grows from about 2' tall by 1.5' wide in a large container. Produced about 25 small, round fruit per plant.

'Cayenne Chili Peppers': Hot pepper that grows from about 2' tall by 1.5' wide in a large container. Produced about 40 small, round fruit per plant.

Dwarf Bell Peppers: Came without a name on the tag (other than dwarf peppers), but did amazingly well. They only grew about 12"-16" tall and averaged 20 small peppers per plant. These plants are quite useful because they are small enough to be tucked into many mixed container gardens. See page 44 for more information.

GROWING CONDITIONS

Light: Full sun, at least 6 hours per day. Don't even think of less!

CHARACTERISTICS

Average Size in a Container: Varies from 1'-5' tall, depending on variety.

Lifespan: 5-7 months

Production: Small peppers produce earlier, with more fruit than the larger-fruited ones. Also, the larger ones sometimes require longer and cooler nights of late summer to produce their harvest. Plant a variety, so you will have plenty. See the list below for individual production numbers.

VARIETIES TESTED

'Red Bell': Gorgeous, great-tasting, sweet, red peppers on a 3' tall by 1.5' wide plant in a large container (at least 16" wide). Highly productive plant, with about 15 peppers. With red peppers costing $2 to $3 each at the grocery store, this variety is a no-brainer.

'Yellow Bell': 3' tall by 1.5' wide plant in a large container. Also highly productive.

'Yummy': A snack sized miniature. My favorite, sweet pepper. Fruit is

 Blue ribbon vegetables are defined on pages 12-13.

Assorted hot peppers

Water: High. I watered daily.

Hardiness: Bell peppers tolerate temperatures from 65-90 degrees, with optimum temperatures ranging from 70-80 degrees. Hot peppers tolerate temperatures from 65-95 degrees, with optimum temperatures ranging from 70-85 degrees; mainly grown in zone 4 and south. Small-fruited peppers mature much faster than the huge ones, so they make a better choice for cooler areas. Bell peppers take a break from producing fruit when the temperatures get quite high but will start up again when the temperatures drop.

The easiest way to find out whether they grow in your area and when to plant them is to check with your local county extension (find their number at www.csrees.usda.gov). Most extension offices can also provide you with a list of varieties that do well in your area. Since there are so many different pepper plants bred for so many different climates, this is a smart move.

Don't rush to plant your pepper plants in spring. Plants that are exposed to too much cold never fully recover.

Propagation: Seeds, but it's easier to buy small plants.

Pest and Diseases: I had no problems at all. Peppers don't have too many pest and disease problems. Look for resistant varieties. I didn't know that any of the ones I grew were resistant, but they certainly fared well!

CARE & HARVESTING

Planting Day: Follow planting instructions on pages 32-35. Use the fertilizer shown on page 36.

Trimming & Supporting: Most peppers need staking to stay upright, especially after they start bearing fruit.

Harvesting: Be sure to check under the leaves because peppers hide! The more you pick, the more the plant produces. Wait until the peppers turn their mature color. Cut off the fruit and a small section

of the stem with scissors. Wash them and put them in your refrigerator. Immature, green fruits often don't taste good at all.

CONTAINER DESIGN TIPS

Container Sizes: Dwarf peppers (about 1' tall) take up very little space. I often tucked them in containers with mixed flowers, and they did quite well in a small spot. Medium-sized peppers (about 2' tall) require larger pots. I recommend at least a 14" diameter. Large peppers (about 3' tall) do best in pots with at least an 18" diameter.

Use: Peppers look pretty good alone. Check out the combo on page 19 to see 4 hot pepper plants in a bright, Mexican pot. It turned out quite well.

I also used peppers as centerpieces for large containers accented with mixed flowers. See a successful example on pages 98-99.

In side-planted containers, I prefer peppers as centerpieces. Their upright growth habit does not look quite right when planted in the side holes, although they grow well there.

Prior to growing peppers, I had heard from some experts that they wouldn't do well with a lot of plants around them because they need quite a bit of space for their roots. I did not find that to be the case. They lived quite happily with flowers planted quite close to them. But, they do much better in larger containers.

Other Tips: Peppers change color as they grow depending on variety. Many go from green to yellow, orange, or red. Both the taste and vitamin content improve as they mature.

Plant Profiles: Vegetables

Spinach

Cool-Season Vegetable

Spinach is one of the most nutritious vegetables (provided it's not overcooked) and quite easy to grow. It was one of the easiest I tried. Once planted according to the instructions on pages 32-35, it required nothing but water. It didn't look great, however, which I quickly remedied by adding flowers. See pages 62-63 to see the transformation from blah to gorgeous! Choose between 2 types of spinach: smooth-leaved (thin, smooth leaves) or savoy-leaved (crinkled leaves that hold up better to cooking).

Smooth-leaved spinach

CHARACTERISTICS

Average Size in a Container: 6" tall by equally as wide. Hugs the ground.

Lifespan: 2-7 months

Production: Plant quite a few plants for large production, as each plant yields enough for just a few meals. Spinach plants are tightly spaced in containers.

VARIETIES TESTED

'Correnta': A crinkly-leaved variety that did extremely well for us. Resistant to many common diseases and slow to flower (which ends leaf production).

GROWING CONDITIONS

Light: Full sun, at least 6 hours per day. Tolerant of some shade, but give it at least 4 to 5 hours of sun a day.

Water: I watered about every 2-3 days, when the potting mix felt dry.

Hardiness: Tolerates temperatures from 25-75 degrees, with optimum temperatures ranging from 60-65 degrees. Spinach can grow in all zones, including as a winter crop in areas where temperatures don't go below 25 degrees. However, spinach is quite temperature and light sensitive, so plant it at the right time of year. Both long days (more than 12 hours of sun) or temperatures that are too high or low cause spinach to flower and stop producing tasty leaves. Luckily, varieties are available for almost any climate. The easiest way to find out when to plant them is to check with your local county extension (find their number at www.csrees.usda.gov). Most extension offices can also provide you with a list of varieties that do well in your region.

In many areas, spinach can be planted in both spring and fall. For spring planting, plant it about 4-6 weeks before the last frost of spring. In fall, plant 6-8 weeks before the first frost of fall. Spinach can overwinter in zone 8 south.

Propagation: Seeds, but it's easier to buy small plants. Spinach is very slow from seed.

Pest and Diseases: Spinach are relatively trouble-free, particularly if you choose disease-resistant varieties, like the 'Correnta' that did so well in my trials.

CARE & HARVESTING

Planting Day: Follow planting instructions on pages 32-35. Use the fertilizer shown on page 36.

Trimming & Supporting: None needed.

Harvesting: There are two ways to harvest spinach: either leaf-by-leaf or cutting the entire plant. If the weather gets too hot and the spinach begins to flower, cut the whole plant. To cut just a few leaves (so the plant is left to keep producing), start with the outside leaves as soon as they are large enough to be used. Spinach tastes best when picked in the morning and immediately put into cold water, which is drained off before storing in plastic bags.

CONTAINER DESIGN TIPS

Container Sizes: Like many cool-season vegetables, spinach does not require huge containers. A medium-sized pot about 10" wide and equally as tall will support quite a few plants because spinach is spaced quite close together, with only about 6" from the center of one plant to the center of the next one.

Use: Most attractive when used as an accent for flowers. See pages 62-63 for a great example.

 Blue ribbon vegetables are defined on pages 12-13.

Summer squash is one of the most satisfying vegetable of my trials because it produces a lot of great fruit quickly. I grew the 'Yellow Crookneck' and was extremely happy with it, except I didn't understand that so many squash were hiding under the leaves, so I missed picking some. Designing with summer squash or zucchini (which shares the same growth habits) is easy because the plants are attractive on their own. Just plant one in the middle of a large, attractive pot, and let it go! The only problem I encountered was downy mildew in late June, which is why it missed a ribbon. See page 43 for more information on this serious pest.

Squash comes in both summer types and winter storage varieties. Most winter squash are too large for containers, so I limited my trials to summer squash and zucchini. Both have edible blossoms that are quite tasty. Blooms are either males or females, with only the females producing fruit. So, you can pick the male blossoms to eat them (See pages 54-55 for photos of the flowers).

Left:'Yellow Crookneck' Squash   Right: Zucchini, which also comes in a yellow form.

CHARACTERISTICS

Average Size in a Container: The two large ones that were successfully tested grew about 4' tall by equally as wide in a huge (27"W x 31"H) container. Smaller in smaller pots. Grows about 18" tall in the side holes of side-planted containers. Smaller squash and zucchini are also for sale. We tested one (zucchini 'Buckingham'), and it grew much larger than I had expected! See page 20 for a photo.

Lifespan: 2-4 months

Production: One plant in a large container (if you pick frequently) can produce 25-40 fruit.

VARIETIES TESTED

'Yellow Crookneck': Fabulous producer.

'Black Beauty' Zucchini': Another fabulous producer!

Zucchini 'Buckingham': Labeled a dwarf, it grew much larger than I expected. See page 20 for photo. Yellow fruit.

GROWING CONDITIONS

Light: Full sun

Water: High. I watered daily.

Hardiness: Prefer a minimum temperature no lower than 50 and a maximum of 90 degrees.

Propagation: Seeds, but it's easier to buy small plants.

Pest and Diseases: Both downy mildew (in humid parts of the county) and squash borers are serious problems. See pages 43 and 54 ('Troubleshooting') for more information.

CARE & HARVESTING

Planting Day: Follow planting instructions on pages 32-35. Use the fertilizer shown on page 36.

Trimming & Supporting: None

Harvesting: Yellow squash is best picked when it is 4"-6" long, before many warts have formed. Zucchini can be harvested when quite small (3"-4" long), or you can wait until they are 6"-8" long. It doesn't matter how much of the stem you get, but be sure to harvest when the skins are still soft. Cut off the fruit with scissors to keep from damaging the plant. Pick them at least every other day. If you miss picking some until they are overripe, remove them from the plant to keep it producing more. The more you pick, the more you get!

CONTAINER DESIGN TIPS

Container Sizes: Understand that most summer squash and zucchini are very large plants and need very large pots to produce large fruit. I liked the container on pages 54-55 best, which measures 27" across! That might have been overdoing it a bit, but the squash loved it. If you want to try a smaller one, stay larger than 16" in diameter - the larger the better.

I also had good luck with both squash and zucchini in the side holes of side-planted containers. The fruit only reached about 3" in length, but it tasted good all the same. Be sure to plant trailing plants above it because both squash and zucchini end up growing straight down, leaving a bare spot above (pages 86-87).

Use: Plant alone in the center of a large container. Most squash and zucchini grow too large to allow small flowers in their space. Or, if you want to combine them with flowers, plant the vegetables in the side-holes of a side planted container, and plant top with flowers. See page 89 for an example.

Plant Profiles: Vegetables

2ND Tomato

Tomatoes are the most popular vegetable in the United States. They are easiest to grow in locations with at least a 4 month growing season and low humidity (although there are varieties for most any climate). I did well with them in high humidity, and I didn't mind spots on the leaves that resulted from that humidity.

Although there are about 25,000 tomato cultivars, they fall into 2 basic groups: vining (indeterminate) and bushy (determinate). Vining tomatoes generally bear fewer fruit at one time, but they bear much longer than the bushy ones. Bush tomatoes bear more tomatoes at once, but they stop bearing after about 6 weeks. The bush tomatoes were easier to control than the vines.

One of the biggest challenges with tomatoes is disease, but diseases are less frequent in containers. Some cultivars are less susceptible than others for your area. Check with your local county extension office for local information (find their number at www.csrees.usda.gov).

Getting tomatoes to look good in containers was another big challenge I faced. The first ones I planted looked just awful, but luckily, I learned five ways to easily create attractive, containerized tomatoes (see opposite page under 'Use').

CHARACTERISTICS

Average Size in a Container: Varies from 1'-5' tall, depending on cultivar. The average, large plant grew 3'-4' tall in my large containers (20" wide). The larger the pot, the bigger they grow. I was able to crowd flowers around them and still get quite a bit of fruit.

Lifespan: 2-5 months

Production: Depends on what type and size of tomato, as well as what size pot. Generally, the larger the plant and the pot, the more tomatoes. Our smallest dwarf yielded about 20 fruit. Our largest cherry tomato bore hundreds.

VARIETIES TESTED

'Better Bush': An excellent, bush tomato that is ideal for containers. Nice, compact growth habit. I used

it as a centerpiece as well as planted in the sides of side-planted baskets. It reached a height of about 2'-3' tall.

'Husky Cherry Red': Great, compact growth habit that produced hundreds of little cherry tomatoes. I used it as a centerpiece. It grew about 3'-4' feet tall in large (20" wide) containers. This is a unique dwarf vining type, so it keeps producing until frost gets in the fall.

'Sweet 100': HUGE! I planted them in the sides of a side-planted basket and placed the basket on a 4' border column (see page 83 for more information about border columns). The plants grew so large that they hit the ground quickly. I didn't realize I could simply trim them at the bottom, so I moved the basket to the edge of a deck where it had quite a bit of room to trail. It ended up trailing a full 8'! Huge plant with a huge number of tomatoes!

'Patio': Sturdy, upright growth habit that did quite well in all my containers, reaching a height of 2'-3'.

'Bonnie Grape': Cherry tomato excellent for the sides of side-planted baskets. More compact than 'Sweet 100.' Used it quite successfully in the side holes of side-planted baskets. Large fruit production.

GROWING CONDITIONS

Light: Full sun, at least 6 hours per day. Don't even think of less!

Water: High. I watered daily.

Hardiness: Plants die in a freeze, so don't put them out until the temperatures are at least 40 degrees at night. Most tomatoes bear fruit ideally with a minimum of 65 and a maximum of 80 degrees, with 70-75 degrees being ideal. Luckily, many vari-

 Blue ribbon vegetables are defined on pages 12-13.

CONTAINER DESIGN TIPS

Container Sizes: I grew dwarf tomatoes in containers with diameters as small as 14" wide; larger tomatoes were grown in pots up to 20" wide by equally as tall.

Use: There are 5 easy ways to get tomatoes to look good in containers:

1. The easiest method is to plant an upright variety all by itself in a nice pot with attractive hardware, as shown on pages 58-59.

2. Surround the tomato with a simple flower border as shown on pages 96-97.

3. Use the tomato as a centerpiece in an arrangement with mixed flowers as shown on pages 100-101.

4. Tomatoes did beautifully as the centerpiece of side-planted baskets, as shown on pages 66-67.

5. Plant them upside down in the bottom planting holes of a side-planted container, as shown on pages 64-65 and 118-119. The tomatoes form a 'skirt' and look best when the basket is mounted on a 4' border column (see page 83 for more information about border columns). Plant long, trailing plants above the tomatoes (like ornamental sweet potato vines) because the tomatoes end up growing straight down, leaving a bare spot above them that is easily filled in by trailing plants.

Other Tips: Keep it simple, and be sure to use attractive pots and hardware. Nice trellises and obelisks look much better than cheap tomato cages. Bush tomatoes are easier to keep looking neat than vining tomatoes.

eties exist for almost any climate, and tomatoes are successfully grown in zone 3 and south. The easiest way to find out when to plant them is to check with your local county extension (find their number at www.csrees.usda.gov). Most extension offices can also provide you with a list of varieties that do well in your area. With 25,000 varieties, it pays to find out which ones do best in your environment.

Propagation: Seeds, but it's easier to buy small plants.

Pest and Diseases: Early blight and late blight are frequent problems, which cause the plants to look ugly and keep them from bearing fruit. Mites are occasional pests. Hornworms can make the plants disappear overnight. Pick them off (they will be about 3" long) if you see them. Be prepared with sprays for the other pests before you plant tomatoes. See page 43 for more spraying information.

CARE & HARVESTING

Planting Day: Follow planting instructions on pages 32-35. Use the fertilizer shown on page 36. Tomatoes are one of the few plants that grow well if planted deep in the potting mix, with at least half of their main stem buried. I didn't try this because I wanted to see what happens if you planted them level or a bit higher than the soil line, and it worked well.

Trimming & Supporting: Books have been written about different trimming techniques for prize-winning tomatoes. I didn't trim mine at all unless they hit the ground from the side-holes of my side-planted containers. Trim them about a foot off the ground if this happens.

I supported all of my tomatoes on trellises or obelisks, regardless of whether they were bushes or vines. Some also required stakes inside the obelisks to keep them upright.

Harvesting: Cut off the fruit with scissors to keep from damaging the vine. Tomatoes can be picked green to keep the birds from eating them and left to ripen in your kitchen. I like to pick mine when they are fully ripe if I'm not having bird problems. Vine-ripened tomatoes generally taste better than those picked too early.

Plant Profiles: Vegetables

Watermelon
Warm-Season Vegetable

Everything I had ever heard about watermelon prior to the trials for this book said never to try them in containers because the vines are too big. However, compact varieties can be grown successfully in containers. We grew the 'Sugar Baby,' which did quite well. See photos and some more information about this success on pages 56-57.

CHARACTERISTICS

Average Size in a Container: Trailed down the edge of the container about 30."

Lifespan: 3-5 months

Production: My watermelons produced one fruit per plant, which is about half the production of the same variety planted in the ground. I planted 5 plants in one container; in total, they produced only 5 watermelon. And mine were small melons, weighing only 3 pounds as compared to 8-10 pounds typical of those grown in the ground.

VARIETIES TESTED

'Sugar Baby': Only variety I tested. This is one of the icebox watermelons, named that way because it is small enough to fit in a refrigerator.

GROWING CONDITIONS

Light: Full sun, at least 6 hours per day. Don't even think of less!

Water: High. I watered daily. Watermelons are quite sensitive to drought. Water very early in the morning so the leaves are dry by the time the morning dew would ordinarily dry. This is to help prevent diseases. Direct the water to the potting mix, which reaches the roots of the plants but not the leaves.

Hardiness: Tolerates temperatures from 65-95 degrees, with optimum temperatures ranging from 70-85 degrees. Needs 2-3 months of heat to produce melons. Don't plant until 2 weeks after the last frost date for your location, and be sure the temperature has reached at least 65 degrees. Smaller watermelons, like the 'Sugar Baby,' do better in cooler locations because they mature faster than larger ones.

Propagation: Seeds, but it's easier to buy small plants.

Pest and Diseases: Fungus and leaf spot diseases are common. Follow the watering instructions given here to minimize risks. Check www.bonnieplants.com for more information on pests.

CARE & HARVESTING

Planting Day: Follow planting instructions on pages 32-35. Use the fertilizer shown on page 36. Fertilization is quite important with watermelons because they are heavy feeders.

Trimming & Supporting: None needed. Let the melon grow down the sides of the pot.

Harvesting: Cut off the melon with scissors to keep from damaging the vine, leaving about an inch of stem. It can be difficult to judge whether a watermelon is ripe. I picked mine too late and they tasted bad. Here are some signs:

1. The watermelon changes from bright to dull green.

2. Rap on the skin; you should hear a low-pitched thud (least reliable!).

3. Mark your calendar the day you see the flowers. The melon should be ripe 35 days later.

4. The small curls (called tendrils) near the stem die back.

There are 5 other ways to tell when the melon is ripe. See www.almanac.com/food/watermelonripe.php or http.gardenweb.com/faq/lists/cornucop/2002071935010165.html for more tips.

CONTAINER DESIGN TIPS

Container Sizes: I used a container 16" and 19" tall. Watermelon containers should be a minimum of 19" tall.

Use: I put 5 plants in one pot and they cascaded over the sides. No other methods were attempted.

 Blue ribbon vegetables are defined on pages 12-13.

Bibliography

Cutler, Karan Davis. *The Complete Vegetable & Herb Gardener.* Hoboken, NJ: Wiley Publishing, Inc., 1997

Crawford, Pamela. *Container Gardens for Florida.* Canton, Georgia: Color Garden Publishing. 2005

Smith, Edward C. *Incredible Vegetables from Self-Watering Containers.* North Adams, MA, 2006.

www.bonnieplants.com

Index

Index